ॐ

This Journal Belongs To

Jennifer Ann Morstad

Date December 23, 1994

ℰᔢ

Brownlow Personal Reflections Collection

And Serve It with Love Recipe Collector
Leaves of Gold Daily Planner
Family & Friends Address Book
For All My Special Days Birthday Book
God's Promises for Every Day Journal
Refresh My Heart Prayer Journal
Perpetual Calenders
Write Ideas Blank Journals

WRITE IDEAS BLANK JOURNAL

Copyright © 1993
Brownlow Publishing Company, Inc.
6309 Airport Freeway / Fort Worth, Texas 76117

Dear Heavenly father, Today was a very strange day. We had our Christmas party at our youth group. It was very interesting. After that a few guys from youth group and Minette and I went to a Waffle House. It was horable. Lord the way they treated the people their was just awful. An I just wanted to start crying. The worst thing about it is we are all christians and for people to see us that way is not good. They should be able to see christ through us and notice something wonderful about us. I should have done something rather than sit in the corner listening to it all. Its hard coming back from Eastbreak where all the peope who have a relationship with you and praising you to see people who have a relationship with you, but are pleasing the devil. Lord I would just like to

Those who hope in the Lord will renew their strength.
They will soar on wings like eagles;
they will run and not grow weary, they will walk
and not be faint.

ISAIAH 40:31

pray for Matt T, Tony D, Greg?,
Brian N, Chad?, and Jaimien.
Lord I know they all have
you in their life but the
devil is miss leading them.
I just pray that they will
be convicted and see that
their life style is not pleasing
to you. Lord God I also want
to pray for my brother. I love
him so much and pray
that he will soon be back
with you. I just want to
thank you so much for all
of my friends and that your
hand will be upon each
and everyone of them with
there decisions and all. I just
pray for S.V staff and you
will put whoever on staff if
it may be Prisilla. I love you so
much Lord. Amen

12-30-94

Dear Heavenly father, yesterday was a very fun day. My sisters, mom, grandma and I went to go see Little Women. It was nice doing something with just the women in our family. Lord when my mom, sister and I got on the subject of my cousins the Lochianos I felt strange. I'm not sure if I'm angry with Mary and Tony or what. I am angry that they took Samanthas money. I don't know what is going on. I think Mary and Tony may be in a cult. Who knows. I'm just worried about the kids. I want to help them out some how but I'm unsure on what or how to do it. Missy is thinking about running away. I want to help her. I think Samantha is the only sane person at the house. Lord I just

8

pray for that family
that they will realize
something they are doing
is wrong. Lord I also pray
for my brother. I love
him so much. I just pray
that we as a family can
just get along. I ask that
you could lay your hand
upon Brandon. He is trying
so hard to be Jeff's friend
but it's like Jeff is pushing
him away. I pray Brandon
will continue to have a
friendship with my brother.
You know the reasons why.
Lord I thank you so much
for my sister Krista. I am
so blessed you put her
in my life. She keeps me
accountable and better yet
I look up to her because
of her love for you. It's
so amazing. Lord you are
so amazing. I thank you
for every thing in my
life. Amen.

8a   1-1-95

Dear Heavenly Father, Lord I thank you so much for the trials you put into my life. At times it's hard for me to understand why you put them in my life because they are horrible, but your just trying to help me yield to you. Lord I just pray for the New Year.

I pray that the christians at our school can take a stand for you. I want our school to be on fire for you Lord God. I would just like to pray for Jessica Franco, Lord I'm not sure what is going on but I ask that you would give her strength through her trouble some times. I would also ask that you lay your hand on Rahell. I'm not sure what is going on but her manager seems to be more important in her life right now. Lord I pray for my brother

and his new year that
you would lead him in
the right direction. Amen
1-2-95

Dear Heavenly Father, Today,
was a good day I did not
do much, but this morning
I heard my brother listening
to Wes king which is a tape
of mine. I did not get mad
because he did not ask me,
I got excited that he was
listening to christian music.
It may not mean a whole lot
but it was encouraging. I
found out today that Karen
talked Jeff into going to
a Rock on confrence Lord
I Thank you for Karen and
I also pray for her. She is
going through some difficulties
which you know but I
pray that you can show
her what to do. Lord I
just pray that we are all
ready to go back to school
and Take a stand for

our school. Help us to remember
you in our decisions. Lord
I pray for my brother that
you would just speak to
him this year. I love
you with all of my
heart. Amen.

1-3-94
Dear Heavenly Father, well today
was an interesting one. I found
out so many disturbing things.
It's hard for me to deal with
them. I'm not real sure what
to do. I know my brother hates
me and I don't know why.
I love him so much. I'm not
sure if he knows I care for
him so much and would do
a lot for him in his defence.
But if I were to do so I'm
afraid he would get even

*You will find, as you look back upon your life,
that the moments when you really lived
are the moments when you have done things
in the spirit of love.*

HENRY DRUMMOND

more hatered for me. I don't know.
Lord please just take control
of that situation. Lord I am
also concerned for Karen.
I talked to her briefly this
evening and while I was
talking to her I was dis-
turbed. She was high again.
I don't know what to do.
I care for her and pray
that she would stop but
she would be the one who
wants to change it for
herself. But I do pray for
her. I thank you so much
for my parents They love
me so much. Their love
for you is also so awsome.
Even though I don't show
it a whole lot I love them
dearly and i'm glad you put
my family in my life.
Lord please put your hand
upon my brother. I love
him as much as you do.
Amen.

80

1-4-95

Lord Heavenly Father I am so
thankful for you Lord. Today
was a very good day. I talked
to Karen and gave her some
good verses that I hope will
help her out along her walk
with you. I am so grateful that
my sister was here. She helped
me out on what to say.
Lord I just pray she gets
her life back on track with
you. These past few days back
at school have been awsome.
I feel your love is shinning
through me and I'm making
it apperent. I'm happy and
I love to show it. Thank you
Lord. Heavenly Father I thank
you so much for Melinda.
She is such a great gal.
Her love for you just keeps on
growing. It is a great encouragment.
Please be with my brother
tomarrow and I pray it will
be another great day based
upon you! Amen

What, then, shall we say in response to this?
If God is for us, who can be against us?

ROMANS 8:31

1-5-95

Dear Heavenly Father, Lord
the friends that you have
given me are such a blessing.
Thank you lor God. Today
was a good day, I'm still
concerned about Karen. She
did not go to youth group,
because she "went out."
Maybe it was not to get high.
You only know. Lord I just
would like to pray for my
husband. I have no idea
who he may be but I
just ask that you would
have your hand upon him
and that his love for you will
continue to grow stronger.
Today my friends 3 I just
sat around read favorite
verses to each other. It was
awsome. Mine Nahum 1:2-4.
Lord put your hand upon my
brother. I love you. Amen

1-4-95

Dear Lord, what an interesting
day you have brought upon me.
I quite don't understand Karen.
I love her to death but all I
can do now is pray for her.
She came to school high. I
was unsure on what to do. I
know it was a test. I was
kind of afraid to make eye
contact with her. I don't really
know why. Lord today I found
out some news that has
just devistated me. Ranell. I had
a very long talk with her.
She is very confused. I did
not really have any answers
for her I just kind of
listened. She does not know
if she would rather follow you
or if she would follow her
friends(non-christian) That makes
me so freightened. Why... why
Satan I know this is all
Satan's fault and I hate him
for it. She is so confused.
Lord after we talked I walked

her to the door and when
I shut the door behind
her I just broke down into
tears. I went to the couch
and just cryed. I thought
to myself. There is a
spiritual Battle going on right
within our Bible study. That
is what scares me so much.
Lord I just pray that we
can overcome all of our
temptations. I pray that
Ranell will soon get back
on track and will stay that
way. I also pray the same
for Karen. I thank you so
much for Minette. She has
put up with me and has
helped me so much with
my relationship with you.
Today was her Birthday.
I again pray for my brother
I love him dearly and
pray that he will soon
like me. Amen.

8⃝

1-7-95

Dear Lord, You are so amazing. Everything is so awsome because of you. Thank you. Today was not a big eventful day I went to my grandma's for lunch came home and talked to my friends. Lord I thank you for Melinda. She is just a great friend. She knows what my feelings are. Thank you for putting her in my life. I would like to pray for Kathryn Wegner. She is going to sing tomarrow at church and I pray that you will place your hand on her and help her to concentrate. I love her so much. She is a neat friend. I am so pleased you put her in my life. Lord I pray for Jeff that he will come to know you again. I thank you for my brother. I care and love for him deaply. I love you with all of my heart. Amen

1-8-95

80

Dear Lord, today my sister went back to school. She had been here for 3 weeks. I did not get annoyed when she was here it just felt like she has never been at school. But now that she is gone I miss her. It has not even been a day. I love her a lot I guess that is the reasoning behind it. Lord I want to ask that you will help me tomarrow. I am going to give Ranell a paper with encouraging verses. I have a feeling that she may get a little mad. But as it says in Ezecial 3:18-21 we need to help those in need. I ask that I can stand strong even through that troublesome period. If there is one. In my devotion time this evening I learned that you don't want us to give things up for just giving them up. I just mark you for my brother. He helps me out a lot financialy. I still pray that he will come to know you as his personal Lord and savior again. And I pray for Priscilla and her decision to come on staff at Broomfield. I pray it might be for Broomfield, but if not it is in your will. I pray for my friends that they will not grow weary. I love you with all of my might. Amen

1-9-95

Lord what an awkward day you have given to me. Lord I hate this spiritual Battle so much! Tonight after I got home from S.V. My brother Mom and I got into an argument. My brother went off on the way christians live should be up to themselves. Why does he not understand the way of the bible is the right way

Life's greatest tragedy is to lose God and not to miss Him.

F. W. NORWOOD

I knew tonight was going to be interesting when I found out he was going to have dinner with Jenica Helwig. I have reasons to believe that she has something to do with my brother changing his view on you. Jeff used to have such an awesome relationship with you and stick up for what he believed. But when she gave him that Inherit the Wind movie I knew it was going to fall from there. I just pray for him. I love him even though he may not think.

I also pray for our family we are going through a rough time with the job situation who knows if my dad will have a job tomorrow. Please put your hand over our family and protect us. I love you with all my heart and that will never change. Amen.

1-14-95

Dear Lord, wow what a week
I have had. This week has been
one of the most difficult for
me. On Wed. Ranell, Melinda, Minette
and I decided to turn in Karens
name for doing drugs. Well we
thought it would go well. Some
of our other friends did not
really agree with it. Anyway
It felt like we did the right thing
until Karen told us we needed
to watch our backs. Anyway
Monday night my brother and
I got in an argument. We
did not talk 'til Thursday night.
He told me he wants to get
baptized into the Mormon church.
He asked me to go if he does.
Lord I just don't know what
to do. I don't believe in that
religion so I feel if I go I will
support been the religion. Lord
help me to make the right
choice.
Last night Friday I went
to the "Loft" with Melinda.

✤

*The Lord has done great things for us,
and we are filled with joy.*

PSALM 126:3

It sure has changed since I went
there. Well we met a guy
named Eric. He is a nice guy.
Lord I know you put Melinda
and I there and you put him
in our life for a reason. I pray
for Eric and if he does not
know you he will come to
know and except you. Lord I
pray for my family and ~~its~~
the work situation.
I also pray for Melinda. She
has a problem with bitterness.
Please lay your hand on
my brother. You understand.
Thank you for all the trials
in my life they help me
to come closer to you. Amen.
2-12-95
Heavenly Father it has been
a long time since I have
written. So many things have
happened. Lord I pray for
our group of friends.

satan has sure gotten a
foothold on it. I was in a
fight with Stefani for a few
weeks. It was awful. Thank
you for showing me it was
childish. Lord I thank you
so much for Stefani. For
Ranell. I'm not sure what
to do about her. She and her
27 year old Manager are
dating. It's sick. She is only
16. Lord I pray Ranell will
come back to you and see
that what she is doing is
wrong. He just got a divorse
from his wiff. I think he is
messing with her mind. Lord
I pray he will stop all of
this with Ranell. Lord I pray
for Melinda. She has fallen
from you and does not want
to come back to you. I'm
not sure why. Well Lord about
the guy Eric we met. I'm not
sure what is going on. I think
I may have feelings for him
but I know nothing would

82

ever come out of it because
he does not have a relationship
with you. He has made it known
that he would like to go to
church with me. Lord if you
put him in my life I pray
that you would not put
anything in the way of that.
He came to the S.V. Meeting
but due to Melinda
wanting to leave he left
with her. I pray you would
show me that you put
him in my life.
Lord I pray for my family.
My great aunt Mac died
today. I pray we can make
it through all these trials.
Lord steer us in all the
right derections. I love you
with all my heart. Amen.
3-20-95
DEAR HEAVENLY FATHER, IT HAS
BEEN SO LONG SINCE I HAVE
WRITTEN IN HERE! LORD SO MUCH
IS GOING ON AND HAS BEEN
FOR ABOUT A MONTH OR SO.

MY FRIENDSHIPS WITH MY FRIENDS
HAVE BEEN AWKWARD LATELY. I AM
GETTING ALONG WITH ALL MOST EVERY-
ONE. STEFANI AND I ARE NOT TALKING
AS YOU KNOW. LORD I PRAY THAT
WHEN WE TALK WE WILL SORT OUT
EVERYTHING AND STAY FRIENDS FOR-
EVER WITH YOU AS OUR FOUNDATION.
MELINDA AND I ARE GETTING ALONG
GOOD, BUT IT KIND OF MADE ME MAD
WHEN SHE TOLD THE "GUYS" TO
BOULDER WHEN WE WERE GOING TO
GO THE LIBRARY. RANELL IS STILL WITH
CHARLES AND IS NOT SPENDING ANY
TIME WITH US. MINETTE AND I WENT
TO COPPER MNT. AND BREKENRIDGE
ON SATURDAY WITH MOODY'S BIBLE
INSTITUTE AND YOUTH GROUP. THAT WAS
AN ADVENTURE. LORD I THANK YOU
SO MUCH FOR MINETTE! SHE KEEPS ME
ACCOUNTABLE AND I THANK YOU FOR
THAT. LORD I WOULD LIKE TO PRAY
FOR DAVID AND LEE CURTIS. THEY
ARE THE CHILDREN OF GREG CURTIS
WHO MAY BE OUR NEXT PASTOR.
I PRAY THAT IF THEY MOVE HERE
THEY CAN ADJUST TO THE NEW

8a

ADVIORNMENT. LORD I DON'T KNOW
HARD IT IS TO MAKE A TRANSACTION
LIKE THAT BUT I CAN IMAGINE.
LORD I PRAY THAT IF IT IS IN YOUR
WILL, PASTOR CURTIS WILL BECOME
CALVARYS NEW PASTOR. I ENJOYED
HIS SERMON YESTERDAY.
LORD I PRAY FOR MY BROTHER.
I FOUND OUT TODAY THAT HE WAS
SUPPOSED TO BE BAPTIZED ON SAT.
BUT DID NOT. LORD I KNOW YOU
ARE THE ONE WHO MADE JEFF
PUT BACK THE DATE ON HIS
BAPTIZM. I PRAY YOU WILL SHOW
HIM THE TRUTH BEFORE IT'S TOO
LATE. LORD I PRAY FOR MY DAD
AND HIS NEW JOB THAT EVERYTHING
WILL GO ACCORDING TO YOU.
LASTLY I PRAY FOR ERIC. I PRAY
I WILL BE A SILENT WITNESS TO
HIM, THAT THROUGH ME, HE WILL
EXCEPT YOU INTO HIS HEART.
LORD I LOVE YOU WITH ALL OF MY
HEART AMEN.
3-31-95
DEAR HEAVENLY FATHER, THIS SPRING
BREAK HAS BEEN VERY GOOD IN SOME

WAYS AND NOT SO GOOD. I HAVE FOUND
OUT A FEW DISTURBING THINGS. A
GUY THAT I KNOW WHO IS A CHRISTIAN
AND HE AND HIS FAMILY WENT TO
CALVARY CHURCH. ANYWAY I FOUND OUT
HE IS GAY. I'M SO CONFUSED. IT IS HARD
FOR ME TO BELIEVE A CHRISTIAN GUY
COULD BE GAY. ITS AGAINST YOUR WILL.
LORD I PRAY FOR THE FAMILY AS
THEY GO THROUGH THIS STRIFF. LORD
I ALSO PRAY FOR MY FAMILY. MY
BROTHER JEFF IS GETTING BAPTIZED
THIS SATURDAY AT THE MORMON CHURCH.
HE INVITED ME TO GO BUT I'M NOT
GOING TO. I STRONGLY DISAGREE WITH
WHAT HE IS DOING. MAYBE THIS WAS
WHAT HE NEEDED. I KNOW YOU DID
THIS FOR A REASON. LORD I JUST
PRAY FOR MELINDA. LORD SHE HAS
FALLEN SO MUCH! THE SKATER GUYS
HAVE TAKEN CONTROL OVER HER LIFE.
SHE DROPS EVERYTHING FOR THEM.
HER ATTITUDE HAS CHANGED TOWARDS
EVERYTHING; SCHOOL, FRIENDS AND

Be a life long or short, its completeness
depends on what it was lived for.

DAVID STARR JORDAN

YOU. I PRAY THAT SOMETHING WILL HAPPEN THAT WILL LEAD HER BACK TO YOU! I'M NOT SURE IF SHE HAS TRIED POT, BUT I KNOW SHE WANTED TO. I JUST PRAY THAT IF SHE DID SHE WON'T GET ADDICTED TO IT. THIS BREAK I SPENT A LOT OF TIME WITH MINETTE. LORD I THANK YOU SO MUCH FOR PUTTING HER IN MY LIFE. SHE IS SUCH AN INSPIRATION. SHE IS SUCH A GREAT WOMEN OF CHRIST AND IS ENCOURAGING. I PRAY LORD THAT STEPANI AND I WILL START TO TALK AGAIN. I MISS HER FRIENDSHIP. IT SEEMS LIKE WE WILL START TO TALK THEN WE WILL STOP TALKING AND I DON'T KNOW WHY. MAYBE YOUR TRYING TO TELL ME SOMETHING WITH THIS. I HAVE SPENT THE PAST 2 DAYS HERE AT MY GRANDMAS HOUSE. IT'S BEEN KIND OF ODD. SHE KIND OF FORGETS A LOT OF THINGS. I GUESS ITS SCARY. SHE FORGOT HOW TO PLAY KINGS ON THE CORNER WHICH IS A GAME SHE TOUGHT ME. I KNOW SHE IS GETTING OLDER. IT'S JUST SAD. LORD I THANK

YOU FOR BRINGING PASTOR CURTIS
TO OUR CHURCH! I PRAY THAT HE
WILL EXCEPT THE OFFER AND BECOME
OUR NEW PASTOR. HIS SERMONS ARE
SO AMAZING. LORD I PRAY FOR
DAVID AND LEE. I PRAY THAT IF
THEY MOVE OUT HERE IT WOULD BE
AN EASY TRANSACTION FOR THEM. I
THINK IT WOULD BE DIFFICULT TO
HAVE TO MOVE. I PRAY FOR JOY
AND MRS. CURTIS THAT EVERYTHING
WILL GO SMOTHLY WITH THEM.
LORD I PRAY THAT WHEN SCHOOL
GETS BACK IN SETION I WILL
FOCUS MY TIME ON YOU AND
SCHOOL WORK. I LOVE YOU WITH
ALL OF MY HEART! IN JESUS NAME.
4-4-95
DEAR FATHER OF ALL, I THANK YOU
SO MUCH FOR EVERYTHING. I DON'T
GIVE YOU AS MUCH THANKS AS I SHOULD
LORD I PRAY FOR MY BROTHER. HE IS
BEING LEAD ASTRAY. HE HAS BEEN HAPPIER
AND NICER TO PEOPLE. I ASK THAT YOU
WOULD HELP MY FAMILY TO COPE
WITH HIS DECISION. I PRAY RIGHT
NOW THAT YOU WOULD HELP ME

*So we fix our eyes not on what is seen,
but on what is unseen. For what is seen is temporary,
but what is unseen is eternal.*

2 CORINTHIANS 4:18

KEEP MY FOCUS ON YOU. ERIC CALLED
ME LAST NIGHT. I DON'T WANT
ANYTHING TO GET MY FAITH IN YOU
TO DROP. I PRAY FOR ERIC THAT
MAYBE IT BE THROUGH ME OR SOME-
ONE THAT HE WILL COME TO KNOW
YOU IN A PERSONAL WAY.
LORD I WANT TO THANK YOU FOR
EVERYTHING YOU DID WITH STEFANI
AND I. WE TALKED ON SUNDAY
AND WE ARE GETTING ALONG.
I PRAY OUR FRIENDSHIP WILL CONTINUE
TO GROW AND YOU WILL BE THE
CENTER OF OUR FRIENDSHIP!
I PRAY FOR MY SISTER KRISTA.
SHE AND BETH ARE NOT GETTING
ALONG BECAUSE OF BETHS NEW
BOYFRIEND. I PRAY THEY WILL
TALK AND KEEP ON GROWING
IN YOU! I LOVE YOU LORD. AMEN.
4-14-95
Dear Heavenly Father, thank
you so much for everything!

Tonight I went out with Stefani and Karen. It was nice. Stef and I have not done anything for a very long time. Lord I pray that our friendship will continue to grow and that we bring you into our friendship. This week I spent almost all of my time with Melinda. It was nice, but I'm afraid that if we hang out too much something might go wrong. So maybe we should not as much time together. Lord I pray for our family I pray my mom will find a wonderful job that you would put her in. She is having trouble with her current job. Lord I pray for my aunt, uncle, and my cousins. They do not know you and I pray they soon will. I love you. amen.

4-22-95

Dear Heavenly Father, thank you Lord for giving me my family. They are so loving. This past week was kind of odd. I was in a strange mood all week. I acted rudely to some people. Lord please forgive me for that. My brother and Melinda are going to the junior prom together. It is kind of odd that Jeff is going with one of my friends, but I pray that things go well. Lord I pray for Oklahoma. It is in total devastation due to the bomb to the day-care center. Lord I pray that they will get the real people behind this and not acuse the wrong people. I pray that the families will look to you and put their strength in

you. I pray for all my
friends that they would
get back on track with
you Lord. We have all
fallen so much and
we need your strength
Lord. I would also like
to pray for Eric. We
don't talk a whole
lot anymore. I pray
that either through me
or someone else he
will come to know
you in a personal way!
I know it may not
happen while I know
him, but there is some-
one out there to do it.
I pray for my mother
as she goes through
her new job experience
and if you want her
to stay she will. If
not it's in your hands.
I love you with all
of my heart. Amen

82

5-8-95

Dear Heavenly Father, thank
you so much for every
little thing you have given
me. Lord I thank you so
much for giving me my
christian friends. Lord I
pray for my friend April
she is not a christian.
She just moved back from
her moms. April moved
away for a year. The reason
why she came back was
because her and her
mom got in a fight. April
would not tell me what
it was about. At the movies
yesterday she told me she
has a girlfriend. She is
bi-sexual. Lord I think she
is confused. She is only
attracted to one girl and that
is her girlfriend. She does
not find other females
attractive at all. Ever since
I've known her she has
changed for the person she

hang out with. She told me she excepted you into her life because I had a relationship with you. Maybe she really believes she is bi, but Lord I pray you will show me how to handle this. April and I were bestfriends our freshman year of high school, but drifted apart in 10th grade. I don't know why but it feels like once oh hey aprils and my friendship is dead. She left the way I knew her but came back a completly changed person. Its kind of like our friendship never occured. Lord I pray that april will evaluate this through and see if the way she is, is really what she wants or if she is just doing

The only ones among you who will be really happy are those who will have sought and found how to serve.

ALBERT SCHWEITZER

it to please her girlfriend.
She told me she changed
for me. Lord you know
her true heart, speak
to her. I don't agree
with the lifestyle at all,
but she is a friend. Lord
please show me how to
handle this situation.
Lord I love you with all
of my soul, heart, & mind
Amen.

7-10-95
Dear Heavenly Father, You
have taught me so much in
the past month or so. I was
kind of drifting, but ever
since Promise Keepers was
here I have come closer to
you. I have learned so much.
There is so many strange
things going on it's odd.
Mindie and Brandon are
together I guess you could
say that, but when I
said to her "you and your
boyfriend" she seemed

to not enjoy the sound of
I don't think she likes
commitment. Lord I pray for
their relationship that it will
continue to grow in you
and you alone. I pray for
Stef and Dan, that there
would no longer be any
bitterness between them.
Lord my friendship with
Brandon has kind of changed.
We use to be close and
now its different. I pray
you will guide that friendship.
Lord I believe I am starting
to have feelings for Chris.
I don't think that is very
safe. Amy and K.K. both have
feelings for him. I think if
I also did there would be
some bitterness. Lord I pray
that you would take my
feelings away that I do
have toward him. But if
it is in your will let
it be. I just don't want
to loose any friends over

The grass withers and the flowers fall,
but the word of our God stands forever.

ISAIAH 40:8

H. Lord I pray for my Mother
father and I. We are all
looking for a job opportunity
I pray that you would bless
us all in finding the
right job that you want
us to have. Lord I pray
for all of my friends and
their struggles that they
would cast their burdens
to you. I thank you for
each and every friend.
I love you Lord. Amen.
7-22-95

DEAR HEAVENLY FATHER, LORD I
THANK YOU SO MUCH FOR HELPING
ME YEILD TO YOU. LORD YOU HAVE
BLESSED ME SO MUCH. I THANK YOU
THAT ON 7-11-95 YOU PROVIDED
BOTH MY MOTHER AND I WITH
JOBS. THAT WAS A TOTAL ANSWER
TO PRAYER. LORD TODAY MY FAMILY
COUSINS LEFT. I WAS KIND OF
MEAN TO SOME PEOPLE AND THEY

ARE SOME OF THEM. LORD PLEASE
FORGIVE ME. TONIGHT, MINETTE,
MELINDA, STEFF AND I ALL
WATCHED LITTLE WOMEN. LORD
I THANK YOU SO MUCH FOR MY
FRIENDS. WE HAVE ALL GROWN UP
A LOT IN YOU AND IN ATTITUDES.
YOU HAVE BLESSED ME WITH
SUCH WONDERFUL FRIENDS AND
I THANK YOU SO MUCH FOR
EVERY SINGLE ONE. EACH ONE
MEANS SO MUCH TO ME. LORD
I PRAY FOR THE YOUTH GROUP
COMING BACK FROM MEXICO. LORD
I PRAY THEY EACH GOT SOMETHING
OUT OF THE TRIP AND GREW
SO MUCH CLOSER TO YOU. I PRAY
FOR THE UNITY, THAT WE WILL
NOT BE SEPERATED WHEN THEY
COME HOME. LORD I PRAY THAT
LEE'S AND MY FRIENDSHIP WILL
BE AS IT WAS BEFORE ANYTHING
WAS SAID. LORD AND THAT OUR
FRIENDSHIP WOULD BE TOTALLY
BUILT ON YOU. I'M NOT SURE
WHAT MY FEELINGS ARE FOR HIM
BUT LORD I PRAY YOU WOULD

TAKE THEM AWAY SO I CAN
TOTALY BE FOCUSED ON YOU.
LORD I PRAY FOR THE HANSONS.
I LOVE THEM SO MUCH. PLEASE
LAY YOUR HAND UPON THEM
AND PROTECT THEM FROM THE
DEVIL. THANK YOU FOR EVERYTHING
LORD. AMEN.
7-23-95
Dear Heavenly Father, today
was a good and interesting
day. I spent most of the
day with Minette and
Pat. I had fun. It was
kind of odd. I talked a lot
with Pat. Lord I pray for
him and for the next
week or so. I pray he will
lean to you for his strength.
We are becoming better
friends and I thank you
so much for that friend-
ship. Lord I pray for
Dee and my friendship.
Its been awkward the past
few times we have talked.
I pray that we will

soon be able to be good
friends and carry on as
we use to. I pray for
all those who got back
from Mexico today. I
pray for their strength
and health. Today was
Stefanie birthday. I am
so thankful we are
getting along so well Lord.
We have both grown
up so much. Thank you
for mending our friendship.
I thank you so
much for my family
and my friends. I am
truly blessed with all
of them Lord please
lay your hand upon my
mom she is in a lot
of pain Please give her
strength in all. I love
you Lord Amen.
7-25-95
Lord thank you so much
for my family. I have
not been spending a

whole lot of time with
them lately. I feel bad in
many ways. I think I
should spend some
more time with them.
Please help me to keep
that a main priority.
Today was a fairly
good day. Minette and
I are kind of distant.
A lot of that is because
of me. I just find that
she has changed a lot
since this whole Brandon
thing. Brandon has changed
a lot to. For some reason
its hard for me to be
as open with him as I
use to be. We have
hardly talked since he
got back from Mexico. I
completely understand he
has other priorates but
I just feel things
have changed. The one
thing I am afraid of is
him telling Minette

certain things. I know
he has told me he
wouldn't, but I know
things would probably
we said. I love Michelle
to death, and I tell her
almost everything, but
there is some things that
I don't. God I also
pray for David. I don't
exactly know what is
going on with him. I pray
you will lay your hands
upon him and show
him that you are everything.
I pray for Ranell and
everything we talked about.
and I know one day
she will truly except you
and live her life for
you. I pray for all of my
friends going through
trials that you will guide
them closer to you Amen.

*Let us not go faster than God. It is our emptiness
and our thirst that he needs, not our plentitude.*

JACQUES MARITAIN

7-26-95 Dear Heavenly father,
Lord there is something I
am very worried about. I have
this odd feeling that there
is going to be an argument
within the youth group. It
might be because of me. I don't
know for sure, but I think
Trisha and Natalee might be
angry with me for what I
said to Lee. Lord I pray that
they would not be bitter
with me. I don't know my
feelings towards Lee, but
Lord if things are not want
you want, please take
whatever feelings away. I
pray that our group will
not fall apart. We just started
getting close, but I know that
if you feel we need a trial
right now, you will give
us one. Lord I have been
in a odd mood for awhile.
I was rude to both Brandon
and Minette. Please forgive
me. I have also been rude

to my sister. I don't know
why. I don't mean to. Lord,
please help me to control
that area. I pray for Chad.
I'm not sure where he is
at spiritualy, so I pray he
will continue to grow closer
and closer to you. I don't
know what is going on with
this whole Chad thing. I
know I may have some
kind of feelings for him
but I don't know. Lord please
show me how to handle
that situation. I thank you
so much for everysingle
one of my friends. I love
them very much. I love you
with all of my heart. Amen.
7-27-95
Heavenly Father, thank
you so much for today.
It was an interesting
day. I was sick for the
most part. But other
than that it was a
good day. Brandon and

In God I trust; I will not be afraid.
What can man do to me?

PSALM 56:11

I talked a lot today.
It was really good.
Melinda told me she
thought Pat was showing
he liked me. Lord if
he does I pray you
would take those feelings
away. I do not feel the
same for him at all.
Lord I thank you so
much for Mindy. I
had been treating her
differently for some
reason. I don't know
why but I hope she
knows I love her
as my sister in christ.
I pray for those in
our group who are not
close to you that they
will grow closer to you
and not get into any-
thing they shouldn't.
I thank you too

much for my sister
she is so awesome
and very encouraging.
Lay your hand on
her and protect her.
Thank you Lord. I
love you with all of
my heart. amen.
7-30-95
Dear Lord, something is
wrong with me today.
I dont know why. I
was taking everything
he said to me so
seriously. I dont know
if I should have or
not. he has been very
awkward towards me
ever since that night
I told him. Lord I pray
he will find it in just
be nice to me, if he
hates me let me know
so I can go on. I've
never really let it get
to me before. Lord
help me to control

48

my mood swings. They
are so out of control
I pray for all of my
friendships and the
ones to come ahead.
Lord I pray for Eric.
If he does come back
that we can become
better friends than we were
before. I pray for our
group that you will
stay our focus and
that we will lean
to you for everything.
Thank you Lord Amen.
8-8-95
Lord I thank you so
much for my friends.
The past few nights
have been amazing.
Lord I pray for
Brandon and his mom
that they would sort
out their differences.
I thank you so much
for Brandon. He is
one of my closest

49

friends. Thank you
for bringing the friend
ship that I've have.
Lord I pray for David.
He is a little strange
I just hope he will
open up and become
good friends with a
lot of the people in
our group. I pray for
my family and their
relationships with
you, that they continue
to grow. Thank you
so much for life.
amen.

8-9-95
Dear heavenly father today was
kind of a tuff day for me.
I do not understand Lee. We
always seem to fight. I hate
it. We are two totally different
people. Lord please help me on
what to do about this. All
I want to do is stop
talking to him and let life
go on. But I know he is

my brother in christ and through you we should make things work out. Tonight we got in a fight because he swore. He told me it was just as bad as me talking about sex all the time. Maybe it is. Lord from this point I am going to try not to joke around about that. I thought I made myself clear that I would not have sex untill I was married. But the fact was it was not glorifying to you. Lord please forgive me and help me to not speak about that. I am so thankful for my friends. Stef, Minette, Mel, Brandon, and Amy are my closest friends right now. I love each one of them to death. They care about me so much. Thank you so much Lord for putting every single one of my friends in my life.

We have all come so far.
I pray that AJ and I can
continue to have a strong
friendship. And I pray for
our group. If anyone is
bitter towards anyone else
in our group that they
would go to you and get
it all worked out. All the
friendships mean so much.
I pray for your protection
that as school starts we
all will still be close and
growing closer every day.
And thank you so much
for every little thing. My
parents are a totall gift
from you, thank you for
them. I pray for my bro
and sis's. You would just
protect them from everything.
Lord I love you so
much I could never express
how much. I love you. Amen.

Wherever there is a human being,
there is an opportunity for kindness.

SENECA

8-14-95

Dear Heavenly Father, Lord
I lift up Jessica to you
right now. She has gone
through 2 brain surgeries
since 8-12. They found a
blood clot the size of a
tennis ball in her brain
The doctors removed part
of her brain. She is now
in a drug enduced coma.
Lord just keep your healing
hand upon her. I thank
you so much for the
health of my family
and friends. We often
take things for granted.
Lord I pray for the
next school year. For
Steph and I that we
would not get in any
arguments, and if we
do that we would bring
them to you. Let us
be mature in all of
our thinking.
I pray that all of the

youth group would not stop growing in friendships and in you Lord. That as temptations arise, we will listen to you and only you. I pray that our peers will notice a change in our group, that we are loving and have the love of you within us. Lord I did not talk to my non-christian friends at all this summer. I pray we will still have a friendship but I would stand strong in my convictions. I love all of my friends and thank you for them. I pray for my family. For my dad that you will bless him with a job. And for my bro that he would pursue being a christian, for my mom the strength for her job, my sister

But thanks be to God! He gives us the victory
through our Lord Jesus Christ.

1 CORINTHIANS 15:57

Krista a blessed school
year and new experiences
and for my sister
Kari and brother in
law Rick that they
would soon come to
know you in a personal
way. I thank you for
blessing me with such
a wonderful family.
Thank you so much
for grandma Helen. She
is such a blessing.
Lord I love you so
much. Thank you for
everything. Amen.
8-16-95
heavenly father I want to
thank you for answering a
prayer of mine. Lee and I
talked the other night. we
decided we would make
a new start with our
friendship. He came up

to Me and told Me he
did not hate Me and that he
just jokes around a lot. I
pray that we can have a
friendship that will glorify
you. Thank you Lord for
being who you are and for
letting Me feel your presence.
In your sons name Amen.
8-20-95
Dear Heavenly Father, Lord you
have been teaching Me so
much about life these past
few days. Today at 11:00 A.M.
Jessica died. The doctors
took her off the resperator
last night. She did not have
any brain function left. Lord
I pray that she is having
a Marvelous time with you.
I know she is in a Much
wonderful place now. She will
be Missed but her friends
and family will see her
soon. I also found out
that a guy that I went
to school with died a

few days ago. His name
was Tom Balkwey. I did
not know him a whole
lot, but I knew him. He
was in my class. Lord I
pray that this will show
others to not drink and
get high. Tom died by
falling out of a tree
because he was intoxicated
Lord I pray for his family
that they would come to
know you in a personal
way through this trial.
Lord I would also like
to pray for my spanish
teacher Mrs. Roberts. I heard
tonight that her husband
died while they were climbing
a mountain together. I don't
know if it's true or not,
but Lord if it is I pray
Mrs. Roberts would also
come to know you through
this.
Lord I pray for Melinda.
Her faith is not doing

so well right now. Please
put her focus back on
you and help guide her
into keeping a consistant
relationship with you Lord.
That nothing will distract
her now Lord. I pray
for Krista. She has not
had a great week at school.
Please keep your hand upon
her and keep her from
harm. Lord I love you
so much. Please be with
Jessicas family as they
go through this difficult
trial. Lay your hand
upon them. Thank you Lord
for every trial and thing
you show us. I love
you. Amen.

9-11-95
Dear Gracious Heavenly Father,
Lord I thank you. Your
love seems to grow stronger
every day. You are so
amazing. Lord you have
taught me so much

in these past two days
its amazing. I can feel
your presence surrounding
me. Thank you Lord.
I am so thankful you
told me to continue to
attend Student Venture
activities. I feel I need
to hold on to S.V. because
it is dear to my heart.
Lord I also thank you
for convicting me about
my attitude and the words
that come out of my mouth
Lord I ask that you will
fill me and make me
alive with you inside
of me. Let people know
I'm a women of God.
Lord I pray for Melinda
and Ranell. You only know
where they are right now
in their walk with you
Put your hand upon
them and keep them
protected. I pray for
Minette that she will

want to come back to
S.V. and that her relationship with you grows
stronger. I pray for
myself that you will
help my focus be
directly on you, and let
my actions show it.
I pray for Stly that
through V.P. her focus
will be directed on you.
Thank you Lord for
every little thing you
show me each day.
I love you. amen.

9-25-95
Dear Heavenly Father, you
are such an awsome God
and nothing can be accomplished
with-out you. you are so
amazing. Lord I ask that
you would give me patience
that is one thing I need
to give completly to you.

Were there no God we would be in this glorious world
with grateful hearts and no one to thank.

CHRISTINA ROSSETTI

Lord I pray that you would take total control of this situation with Chad. I sent him a letter today telling him my feelings for him. Lord if you want things to happen and if not I understand it is not in your will. I pray for Mel Lord that through something through you she will come back to you. Thank you so much for being a forgiving God. Please protect my tongue, mind and heart Lord. Do not let Satans decieving lies enter into my body Lord I lift your name to the highest. Thank you for giving us your son. I love you. In your sons name Amen.

10-19-95

Dear Heavenly Father, Lord thank you for your awesomeness. You are so amazing. These past

few days I have been
learning I need to be more
like you. God I ask you
would take control over
my bitterness for things.
Being bitter is so horable
I can't stand it, so
I give you that part
of my life. God please
keep me to be a better
servent to my friends
you have blessed me so
much with my friends
and I seem to be taking
them for granted. I
also ask that you
would help me to be
more submisive to you
Thank you God so much
for every new thing. you
are so amazing! I would
like to pray for Jakes
dad. He suffered from a
heart attack the other
night and I ask you
would protect him and
the family. I also

I have come into the world as a light, so that no one who believes in me should stay in darkness.

JOHN 12:46

would like to pray for Tony and the situation with his family. Lord you know whats going on so I ask you would take complete control over it. Lord it is I know you are doing it for the best, I pray that Tonys relationship with you will grow emensly. And God I pray for Melissa. She is such an amazing girl. Please keep your hand upon and and protect her from Satans lies. God help me to keep my thoughts and mind on you and you alone. I love you so much. Amen

10-27-95 Dear Heavenly Father, Lord I lift up this situation with Kathryn Wagner to you. I don't understand

why she is spreading
those horrible rumors.
Maybe she isn't and I
am taking it too seriously,
but Lord please take
control! I am going to
try and attempt to speak
to her about it but what
ever you want it will be.
Lord I don't know whats
going on about this whole
Scott thing. Ever since
homecoming we don't
talk Lord I ask that
you would also take control
of that. I lift up Melinda.
She has fallen so much.
We never talk but
Lord keep your healing
hand on her and don't
let her slip away. Use
me as a light for you.
Please help me to over-
come my bitterness problem
I hate it. I want you
and you alone to shine
through me. Thank you

so much for using
Pastor Curtis to disciple
me and those around.
You truly shine through
him. Thank you Lord
for all of my family
and friends. Help me
to be more like you
Lord. I love you. Amen.
11-4-95
Dear Heavenly Father I praise
you so much for using
me as a warrior for you.
Today I spent the day
with Melinda. It was the
first time since August we
have done something together.
She told me she missed us
and wanted to start hanging
out with us again. Thank
you Lord for answering my
prayer. Lord I pray she will
want to come back for good
and start going to church
again. I pray for myself
that satan will not get
a foot hold and bring me

down trying to help Melinda
come to where she use
to be. She is such a
wonderful girl Lord and
I know you can use her
in so many things. Thank
you so much for the
opportunity for the two of
us to get together. I pray
also when she gives
a note of apology to Stef,
Stef will be forgiving
and excepting Lord Please
start softening Stefs heart.
Please help the entire
group be excepting of Mel's
wanting to come back
into the group.
I pray for my extended
family that even we will
be witnesess for you and
that they will come to know
you. Thank you for your
amazing wonders. I love
you! Amen

11-9-95

Dear Heavenly Father, Lord
you are so wonderful. I thank
you so much for my
parents. They are so wonderful
You truely blessed me with
them. Thank you Lord for
giving me the opportunity
to meet new people. I
pray that you will shine
through me and use me
as a deciple. I pray for
Joel and Shane that they
would come to know you
and continue to attend
church functions. Lord I
pray that you would
take the bitterness I
have and fill it with
your love and warmth.
Please continue to work
in my life. Thank you
for everything Lord. Amen

12-8-95

Dear heaveney father,
wow what a week. So
many things seemed

to go wrong. The thing
with K.K. has gotten
worse. She continues to
call me things that
I will not repeat.
God please take total
control over this. I am
so drained from this
whole situation. God
please soften her heart.
I still love her as
my sister in christ.
I never will stop. Give
me the strength and
help me grow closer
to you. I thank you for
Jake.He has been wit
nessing to Joel and
Shane and they excepted
christ on 12-1. God I pray
for Joel. I know I have
feelings for him, but
God you know whats
not. I seem to like

a new guy every other day. Thank you for making me wait until you know who is best for me. Lord thank you so much for Pat. We talked until 1:00 A.M. today. I am so thankful for his friendship. It seemed as if we were not as close as we use to be. I know we were not. I praise you for giving me the opportunity for allowing us the chance to talk tonight. I also pray for Minette and Brandon. Lay your hand upon their relationship. You know whats best for them, so what ever your will let them know. Thank you Lord for being faithful. I love you. Amen.

12-12-95
Dear Heavenly Father, what a week. God, I'm not sure

69

if I made the right decision.
Someone on the S.C. prayer
chain offered to give me the
to pay for fastbreak. I
turned it down. I'm not
sure why. Lord I pray you
will give me a wonderful
opportunity to do something
great over Christmas break.
I pray when Danny comes
that things will go great. In
your sons name amen.
12-19-95
Dear Heavenly Father, Lord
I thank you so much
for this past month or
so. I have had a lot of
hard situations, but you
have helped me through
those. Lord I thank you
so much for Stefani.
we have grown so close.
I pray it will continue
to grow. She has helped
me out so much
with the whole K.K.
thing and everything

✢

The Lord does not look at the things man looks at.
Man looks at the outward appearance,
but the Lord looks at the heart.

1 SAMUEL 16:7

I love her so much, it's like she is one of my sisters. Well I guess she is. I thank you so much for her. I have been spending a lot of time with Jake, Steph, Shane, Joel, Melissa, Tony and Brandon. It's been cool. Lord I pray you will make our group closer. I love each one of my friends so much. Thank you for blessing me with all of them. I've been talking with Dave Jhonson a lot lately. I don't know him all that well, but from what I do know he is a great guy. I pray he will continue to hang out with all of us.

I got a letter from Chad today. I don't know what the deal with him is. He seems to have changed a lot lately. He cursed in the letter which he never has done before. I don't understand him. I thank you for not allowing it to be. The two of us together

1-1-96

Dear Lord, well a new year is upon us. Lord I pray that this year is so amazing that your love will start to flow out of our church youth group. Like Curtis said, "if we don't love everyone, how can we love God." Thank you so much for Curtis Lord. I have had some problems with him in the past. He is a great youth pastor and I have taken that for

granted. I pray for
Melinda and Kanell
that this year they will
come back around and
fall in love with you.
I also pray for Shane
and Joel. They did not
hang out with us
much this break. I pray
you will keep your hand
on them and protect
them for the worldly
distractions. Please bless
this year and fill it
with trials, tribulations,
joys, blessings and new
relationships. You are
such as awesome God.
I love you so very
very much. Thank you
Lord for your love. Amen.

1-6-98
Dear Heavenly Father. Today is
Minette's birthday. We had a
party for both Minette and Pat.
Thank you Lord for the both
of them. They mean a great

of my friends. Lord you are
so amazing. You have blessed
me and my family. Thank
you Lord. Krista went back
to school today. I already
seem to miss her. She
is so amazing. Thank you
for using her. I love
her so much. I love
my entire family! Mom
dad, Kari, Krista, Debb and
Grandma. I pray for
grandma. She is ill. Right
now. I have a feeling
she will be "going home"
soon. Lord she is in your
hands now. Thank you for
giving me such a terrific
grandmother! Something has
been wrong with me the
past few days Lord. I don't
know what it is. Maybe
it's the way Danny treated
me when he was here.
He never kept any promises
and never said good bye.

That made me upset, but
more than anything hurt.
I know we have both
changed so much, maybe
that's why he did not
want to be around me.
I guess I was disappointed
into how he is now, but
he will always be the
Danny I grew up with.
Maybe I'm acting different
because I know grandma
will not be here much
longer. God whatever it be
please give me peace
about it. You are such
an awesome God. Thank
you God for caring for
everyone the way you do.
I know I could not do
it. That's what make you
such a awesome God. I
love you God. Amen.
1-16-9 ?
Dear heavenly Father -
God what a wonderful
week you have given

to me. This past week K.K. and I worked everything out. We are friends again. Then on Friday night, Jeff prayed outloud at the prayer party and just broke down. It was so encouraging when he wanted to go to church on Sunday. God I pray you will still keep your hand upon him. Help him not get away. Thank you God for being so faithful. Those are two prayer requests I had in the past. You have taught me to have faith in you, I just need patience. You are such an awesome God. Thank you God. I love you with all my heart!

2-27-96

Dear God, thank you for the trials you have put into my life this past month. I praise you for bringing Brandon's friendship back to me. Tonight my bird we have had for about 15 years is dieing. It was so strange to hold it in my hands and watch it die. It has not yet but we expect it to. I pray for the glory of friends and that you will protect them from Satan and things which are not pleasing to you. I called April tonight. I have not talked to her for several months. She was not home, so we will see. I love you God! Amen.

3-8-96

Heavenly Father I give you everything that is troubling me right now. I'm not sure what my feelings are on the fact Stef, and Dan may get back together. If they do, God I pray they will not get even close to how physical they were before they broke up. I lift up Brandon. He has fallen so much. I pray he will get the desire he once had will come back. I pray that Minette will not get back together with him, because if she does, he will bring her down. Give me the strength God. I love you so much amen.

The Lord himself goes before you and will be with you; he will never leave you nor forsake you. Do not be afraid; do not be discouraged.

DEUTERONOMY 31:8

3-22-96

Dear Heavenly Father, Please forgive me for not being the child of God I need to be. I have been rude to many people. That is not what I need to be. I need to let people around me know I am different by the prayers I said. God I pray for those in our group. We have all fallen so much. Some more then others. I lift Brandon up to you. He does not seem to want to come back to you. I pray that your will, will be done. I pray for Minette I think she did doing and saying some thing because she is hidding from the truth. I have

had many talks with
her about confronting others.
Like the story in
Galations 2:11-14 when Paul
was against Peter in what
he was displaying by his
actions, and he, thing
confronted him. God please
help me and tell me
wethers or not I should
confront people. I know we
are commanded to, but
help mee to do it at
the right times. Last night
at youth gurup the speaker
talked about how satan
was darkening our nysion
by different things. For
me I believe its the way
I am so nigative towards
myself, I always tell my-
self, "oh your ugly, you
need to loose weight, your
so white, nobody will
ever want to be with me."
God you made me in your
image and I am very

blessed for that. satan
speaks the lies and you
speak the truth. Lord
thank you for loving me
for who I am. I lift
up my friends. They
mean so much to me
and I have not shown
it at all for the past
month or so. They are
all so dear to my heart
and if it were not for
you I would not have
them. Thank you Lord.
I pray for my attitude
that it would be a Holy
one and the things that
come out of my mouth
would build others up and
not tear them down. convict
my heart Lord when I
start talking bad about others.
As it says in Eph 4:29
"do not let any unwholesome
talk come out of your
mouth." Please guard
my heart, because what

is on ones heart is what
comes out of their mouth.
I pray that this spring
break will be such a
spiritual awakening for
all of us. We all need
to put our focus back on
you. I pray for Chad. The
last letter I recieved from
him was in December.
In the letter he cussed.
It made me angry so
I did not end up writting
him back until about a
month ago. I know I
should have written him
back sooner, but I didn't.
Hopefully he will write me
back soon. Either way dad
I ask you will protect him.
I'm not sure where
he is spiritually, I don't
need to know, but I pray
he will continue to grow
closer to you. God you are
such an awesome dad.
Thank you for all the

wonderful blessings you
have given to me through
out the years. Help to guide
me in the direction you
want me to go. I love
you with all of my soul.
amen.

8-23-96

DEAR HEAVENLY FATHER, I AM
SITTING HERE WAITING FOR STEFANI
TO CALL. I BELIEVE SHE WENT OUT
WITH DAN. WE WERE GOING TO DO
SOMETHING AT ABOUT 10:00 TODAY, BUT
THEN SHE CALLED AND SAID WE
WOULD GET TOGETHER AT 3:00. WELL
IT IS 15MIN. UNTILL 4:00. SHE HAS
PROMISED THAT NOTHING WILL CHANGE
IF HER AND DAN GET BACK TOGETHER.
BUT THINGS HAVE ALREADY CHANGED
SHE WANTS TO SPEND ALL OF HER
TIME WITH HIM. THATS GREAT AND ALL
BUT I'M AFRAID SHE WILL NOT WANT
TO SPEND TIME WITH ME AND JUST
SPEND IT ALL WITH DAN. LORD I PRAY
THAT IF THEY DO GET BACK TOGETHER
THAT THEY WILL NOT BE AS PHYSICAL AS
THEY WERE WHEN THEY USE TO BE

83

TOGETHER. THEY HAVE ALREADY KISSED SEVERAL TIMES AND THEY STILL ARE NOT TOGETHER. MANY PEOPLE IN OUR GROUP ARE THAT WAY. WE ARE SUPPOSED TO BE DIFFERENT FROM THOSE WHO DO NOT BELIEVE IN YOU.

3-24-96

Dear Heavenly Father, well I stopped there because Stef showed up at my house. She was about an hour late. God I'm afraid. I'm afraid that its going to start happening again. The arguments Stef and I use to be in at months at a time. I'm not sure why I feel this. Maybe I'm going to be jealous of the time they spend together. Like I said yesterday she has already started to break plans with me. Whats going on. I feel as if all my friends

We have a God who delights in impossibilities.

ANDREW MURRAY

are abanding abandoning me.
Maybe you're trying to tell
me something Lord that
I need to put all my
trust and energy in you.
are you trying to tell me
I have abandond you? Is
this a taste of my own
medicine? Lord please help
me to rely on you and
only you. Please help me
to speak up when I
know it is not uplifting to
others. Lord I thank you
so much for helping
me control my "hormones"
etc. I have a feeling
Tony did not want to go
to the movies with me
because he knew I would
not put out or give him
anything. Thank you Lord
for instilling that in
me. I pray for Tony
because all he seems
to want is to be
close to a girl. Lord

help me to keep those
strong morals. It is not
right to do sexual things,
such as a kiss, when
you are not even with
somebody and even then
its hard to say unless
your married. I pray for
Minelle. She continues
to be with Brandon
all the time. She is
not helping herself. I
ask God that you would
do something drastically
fast if it be in your
will. I also pray for
Melissa. Our friendship
has not been the
same for awhile. God
I pray for her and
what ever she is going
through. Protect her God.
She has got such a
wonderful heart. I pray
you will start to bless
me with more Christian
friends. I love all of

*I love the Lord, for he heard my voice; he heard my cry
for mercy. Because he turned his ear to me,
I will call on him as long as I live.*

PSALM 116:1,2

my friends so much,
but none of them are
helping to encourage to
grow closer to you. They
are not keeping me
accountable for things
I need to be held for.
I know its not them
that have to be the
ones who have to make
me grow closer to you,
thats between you and
me. But it is so
encouraging for friends
to hold me accountable,
and for me to keep
them accountable with
out them getting angry
with me. At this moment
I dont have a friend like
that. I do have Krista,
but I need someone.
who I hang out with.

88

Lord please change all of
our hearts. They are corrupt
with all these lies of
satan. He is destroying
our relationships we have
together and with you.
I pray in the name of
Jesus, satan get out of
our Jesus' teritory, you are
not welcome here! You are
such an awesome God.
I life your name on
high. Help me to keep
my eyes focused on you.
I love you Lord Jesus.
In your sons name I
pray. amen.
3-25-96
Dear Hevenly Father, what an
interesting spring break I have
had so far and it's only Monday.
I got a letter from Chad today.
I was very amazed. I did not
think he would write me back
for a month or so. Lord I pray
for my friendship with Chad.
I don't know what the deal

with it is. He does not have
S.U. due to the staff not having
any time. And he does not have
a church that he goes to. I pray
that he will continue to have
faith and grow in you. He has
not said anything in response
to the letter I wrote him about
me having feelings towards him.
I continue to have dreams about
him. Not inapropriate dreams. Are
you trying to tell me something?
Lord I lift up Ranell and
Melinda. I don't talk to them
much. I've only seen Melinda
one time since she graduated
at semester. I don't think she is
doing very well. Ranell is still
with Charles. I pray that their
relationship will not last. Lord I
pray that they will see the
light and your love once again.
I pray for Travis Olsen. He has
coming to youth group for a
month or so. I think he is
still hesitant on becoming a
Christian. I ask that if it be

in your will to put the desire
in his heart to want to know
you in a personal way. He is
friends with Matt. He is the
one who invited Travis to
youth group. I thank you for
Matt and his willingness to
grow closer to you, and to get
his friends to youth group.
I talked to Melissa today. She
still does not sound like herself. Lord please keep your
hand on her. I lift up my
family. They are so awesome. They
all care for me so much. I'm
thankful to have parents who
are believers as well as Krista.
I pray for Jeff, Kari, and Rick
that one day they will except
you as their personal Lord and
Savior and that their lives
would reflect it. I pray for
Grandma. She is such an
amazing woman. She is about
84 but has the heart of a 30
year old. I pray I'm able to be
like that when I am her age.

I also pray for Art. Dads friend.
He has cancer and has only a
few more days to live. My dad
thinks he is a christian. Only you
know Lord. I pray for the family.
Protect them in this situation.
I pray that through this trial
they may come closer to you.
Thank you Lord for being so
forgiving. Amen.
3-26-96
Dear Heavenly Father, Well
tonight was sure interesting.
I went to TNL with Steph,
Jake, Minette, Brandon, Tony,
Kerrie, and Kevin. I don't
understand what is up
with Minette, Tony and
Brandon. They have not
talked to us all break
and have been acting
strange around us. Minette
was being rude, so were
Steph & I towards each
other. I decided to confront
Minette w/ why she is upset
but she said everything

is fine. I don't think she
is telling the truth other
wise she would have
called over break. She has
spent all of her time
with Brandon. I don't get
her she tells me to
keep her away from
him but she can't
stop touching him or
being around him. Every
mind Lord calm my
spirit This is not the
attitude I should be
having. I lift up Tony.
I have lost a lot
of respect of him and
I don't have much left.
all he wants right now
is to have a girl he can
play around with. No
matter who she is. Convict
his heart Lord. Let him
see that you need to be
first in His life again

No one has the right to look with contempt on himself
when God has shown such an interest in him.

Lord I ask that you
would calm my spirit
and renew a right spirit
with in me. I pray that
my fire will be a blaze
for you and not just a
little spark. Fill my every
being with your love, kindness,
generousity, patience, everything
you are God. I love you
Forever and ever amen.

4-4-96

Lord Heavenly father, Thank you
Lord for revealing the things
you have to me. This week
has been awesome. Thank you
for helping me realize I need
to be a servant to you and
my friends. I pray for Melissa
and her family. Her uncle died
on Tue. I pray the family will
lean to you Lord. I also lift
up Minette and Brandons
relationship. I pray they will
make you the center of it.
I pray for Brandons willingness
to come back to you. Help

82

them see when they are getting off onto other things. I pray for Stef Lord. She is having many problems with friends. Take total control over them. Help her to see she can not do it on her own. I pray her relationship with you will continue to grow into something awesome. I did talk with Minette over spring break and there was a lot said. She told me everything. Thank you Lord for using her to help me in my walk with you. I pray for Tony and his relationship with his new girlfriend Karen. All I know is they went out to dinner and are now together. I pray you will be the center in this relationship also. And if they start to get physical you would speak to them at that moment. I pray for all of my friends and other christians that ~~they~~ you will set

thar spirit on fire for you
and that it would be a
roaring fire. You are such an
awesome God. (Fill) me with your
loving Grace. Amen.
4-8-96

Dear Heavenly Father, Lord
I thank you so much
for Curtis and Libby
Fletcher. Curtis has been
our youth pastor for about
2 or 3 years now. We did
not get along with him
much at first but now
am very close to both
he and Libby. You know
the situation with his
job. Lord let your will
be done. Give the family
strength to deal with it.
Much of this has to
do with the direction
the church is going. I
don't like whats going on.
The people seem to be

more interested in the
material side of things instead
of caring for those who need
it and putting you in
front of everything. Lord take
control over the situation.
I know you will do the
right thing. Help me Lord
to decide wheather or not.
I should consider changing
churches. Show me the
right way Lord.
Lord please help the seniors
deal with their stress
level. We only have 18 days
left of school. I have been
so stressed this week and
its only monday. Help us
to all concentrate on you
and what we need to
get done I love you so
much Lord. Thank you for
EVERYTHING YOU HAVE DONE! AMEN
4-14-96
Dear Lord Jesus, what an
interesting couple of days.
This past week was so

83

awful from school to
church and almost buying
a house. You are so
amazing God. You have
shown me so much
in just the past 3
days. Curtis our youth
pastor got fired on Thur.
many people were very
upset. including me.
The elder board decided
to fire him. so I got
upset along with others
at them. Well today
at church Tony sr. told
everyone Curtis was reinstated
and asked everyone for
forgiveness. God please
help me with my
interviews. I still have
towards Tony sr. 3 yr.
yesterday we looked at
a house. We all loved
it. today mom & dad
went to go make up
a contract but we found
out someone had already

done it. Lord you know
where you want us. Help
us to make the right
choice to where you
want us. Help me with
the whole school thing.
I only have 2½ weeks
until graduation and I'm
not wanting to do a
thing. Please Lord help
me to concentrate on
the work that needs to
be done. Give me the
strength throughout the
week. I love you Jesus.
In your awesomeness I
pray. Amen.

5-14-96

Dear Heavenly Father, Lord
I pray you will protect me
from all of satans lies.
I am upset by tears because
I wonder why I am not
beautiful. I thought getting
out of high school and
getting into the college scene
would be different. It's not.

Everyone still "runs" to
Minette, talks to her, fall
at her feet, while I get
the usual "what is your
name again" 2 min. after
I just meet the guy. All
that is going through my
mind is why am I so
ugly, why do I have zits
messed up teeth. I know
I was made in your
image Lord and I need
to be thankful. Satan just
keeps telling me I am
ugly, no one would want
to date me. I know you
are going to bless me
with someone someday, but
I also know you may not
want me to be. Take control
over that situation. Today
I turned in some applications.
Lord please choose where
you would like me to work.
Somewhere where you are
able to use me. Please
help me Lord to decide

80

where you believe I should
go. Mexico, Student Venture/
Promise Keepers I am leaning
toward S.V./P.K. Tell me
where you could use me
most! If I do happen to get
a job, I may not be able
to attend any of them.
You are such an awesome
God. Help me Lord to not loose
sight of your rightousness.
I pray for the "friends."
We never get together as
a group anymore. It seems
to be Stefani and Melissa
are upset with me for
some reason. I don't know
what I did. Lord take
over the situation and do
what you want with all
of the friendships. If you
want them to continue
great if not that is what
you desire. Lord Jesus help

Handle them carefully, for words
have more power than atom bombs.

PEARL STRACHAN

me to become more like
you and to not conform
to worldly things. You
are my Rock. I love you
Jesus. Amen.

6-9-96

Dear Heavenly Father,
Lord why am I not
a consistent servant
to you? You do so much
for me and yet I
hardly give anything
in return. Even at
my lowest I don't
give all my cares to
you which makes
me slip further
than ever. This summer
has not been a great
one. Mainly because I
have fallen so far
from you Lord. I had
not gotten along with
Stefani since about a
week after graduation.
Today at church was
the first time in

82

three weeks. I know you
did it for a purpose.
Help me Lord Jesus
to lean to you in
all things. I pray you
will help me stay
on a consistant
stride. I met a guy
today. His name is
aaron Smith. He seems
to be a nice guy. Lord
I pray that you will
be the center of our
friendship. I pray for
Minette. Brandon has
fallen so far from
you and Minette realizes
it but is so caught
up with him that
she does not mind. Open
her heart Lord Jesus,
let her see that she
needs to have the man
being the spiritual
leader of a relationship.
I ask you will bless
all those in need

゚๑

And we know that in all things
God works for the good of those who love him.

ROMANS 8:28

or just need you. I
love you so much
Lord. I never want
to be as low as
I was. I ask that
you will keep your
angels around me to
protect my heart,
soul and mind. Help
me be a wittness for
you. I love you so much
amen.

6-10-96

Dear Heavenly Father,
I thank you so much
for all the wonderful
things you do for me.
You have blessed me
in so many ways.
I pray for my boss
Jim. I am not sure
if he is a believer
or not. I've been
working here at the

shipping connection for about 3 weeks now. I pray that I will be a wittness for you Lord. Let your light shine through me. Thank you for blessing me with this job. It is through you that I got this job. I hope to be here for awhile, but if that is not in your plans Lord, I will understand. About all the talk of moving. I pray that you will put us in the place where you think you can use us the most. I pray for my fathers job. He is hoping to start working in Denver full time. If that be in your will Lord let it. I also pray Lord that you will help Stefani and my relationship. Be

the center of it Lord.
I pray that you will
soften her heart. She
has so much bitterness
in her heart Lord. Take
that away. Brothers and
sisters in christ should
treat others with respect.
I, to need to work on
that also. Let your light
shine through all those
who believe in you. I
lift up Minette. She
has been such an
awesome friend over
the years. Lord I ask
that if her relationship
with you has fallen
that she gets back on
the right track. And
if it's Brandon bringing
her down show her
that. Let her see that
she needs to have
you the center of a
relationship. I thank
you so much for

Melissa. She is such a
wonderful women for
you Lord. She loves you
with all of her heart
and it is so evident.
She is always wanting
to do your will. I
pray that she will
continue to grow so much
closer to you. I lift up
Bill as to Lord. His heart
is filled with anger
and hate towards the
entire church situation.
Show him that he
needs to be a servant to
you alone and not doing
things to try to go
against people or to try
to win peoples approve.
You know his heart, soften
it. Show him the kind
of man he needs to be
through all of this.
Finally I pray for all
those going to Mexico.
Prepare them to be

messengers for you. And
I pray they give all
of the glory to you
and not to themself.
Thank you Lord Jesus
for forgiving me over
and over again. You are
such an awesome God.
I love you so much
Lord. Amen.

10-14-96
Dear Heavenly Father,
Lord you are so good
to me. Thank you so
much for blessing me
with a great family
and friends. I pray
for all of my friends
right now Lord. They
have all fallen so
much. I really pray
that you will shine
through while in
Mexico and may it
continue when they
come back. I lift
up Melissa to you

Lord... Something is wrong
with her. You know what
it is. I pray that she
will bring it up in
prayer also. I think
it may have something
to do with Tony. If
it be in your will
Lord about their relationship
let it be. I pray for
the Smith family. Mr.
Smith just got a job
at calvary as the music
director. I have kind
of gotten to know his
son Aaron. I would like
to get to know him
better. I pray Lord that
if I start to "like"
him and it not be
in your will to not
do anything that would
reperdime a friendship.

God nowhere tells us to give up things for the sake
of giving them up. He tells us to give them up for the sake
of the only thing worth having—life with Himself.

OSWALD CHAMBERS

you know I've done
that in the past and
I pray that in every-
thing I will look to
you and concentrate on
you alone. If aaron and
I do talk may it
be about you and not
to focus the talk on-
to ourselfs. May your
will be done. I pray
for Jake. I have not
talked to him for a
long time. I pray that
with his job, baseball
and Theresa his focus
does not go astray.
I lift up Kari. I ask
that you will use
Krista and I will be
a light and she will
start to see a difference
in me and that I love
you over all things. Thank
you God for everything.
In your sons holy
name amen.

6-15-96

Dear Heavenly Father, Please forgive me Lord of my sin. I am so selfish. I pray that I will become like you. Everyone left for Mexico today. I made little incouragment cards for all of them but did not give them to them because I did not go see them off. I pray that old friendships would be reconciled. I pray Tony and Stef will put all there past grudges behind them and become good friends again because you are what they both have in common. I also pray that the youth will not get too "involved" with eachother. Let them act as if they could see you standing right beside them. They need to be a light for

ॐ

And my God will meet all your needs
according to his glorious riches in Christ Jesus.

PHILIPPIANS 4:19

you and not for eachother.
I pray for a friendship
with Aaron. I don't think
you want any more than
that. I pray that our
friendship is a strong
one and again that is
passed completely on you.
Give us an opportunity
God to have an indepth
conversation about you and
your awesomeness. I thank
you so much for cheryl.
I pray that we get to
know eachother over this
next week. I pray that
her love for you will
continue to grow and be
apparent. I lift up Mike.
I would ask that you
would help him to be
patient and understanding
about getting into a
relationship. Lord bless

him with someone who
loves you as much as
he does. He needs that.
I pray Lord for next
weekend. It is the Student
Venture Hetaway. I am not
going up there for the
whole time. I believe I am
going to see Chad. I pray
that when we see each
other there won't be any
awkwardness. I ask you
Lord to prepare our hearts
for when we do see/talk to one
another. Maybe its in your
will Lord that we don't
talk. May your will be
done. I also pray for
Chad that if he is
not right with you
that this conference will
open his eyes to see
you and that he needs
to live for you. I pray
that my feelings for
him will not come
back. All I want Lord is

82

to glorify you. Be evident
in my life Lord. I want
others to look at me
and notice I am a light
and a child from/of you.
Help me to concentrate
on your word Lord. I love
you! Amen.

6-18-96

DEAR HEAVENLY FATHER, LORD PLEASE
FORGIVE ME WITH MY ATTITUDE. I
HAVE NOT BEEN THAT GREAT OF A
WITTNESS TO OTHERS BY THE
ACTIONS I'VE PROTRAYED. I GOT IN
A ARGUMENT WITH MY MOM LAST
NIGHT OVER THE SIMPEZEST THING
THAT I SHOULD NOT HAVE GOTTEN
UPSET OVER. I WAS BEING SELFISH,
WANTING EVERYTHING MY WAY
OR NO OTHER. LORD HELP ME TO
CONTROL MY TEMPER AND BEING
SELF CENTERED. TODAY IS MY DADS
BIRTHDAY. LORD I THANK YOU SO
MUCH FOR HIM. I'M SO BLESSED
THAT YOU GAVE ME HIM AS
A FATHER. HE TURNS 50. I PRAY
THAT HIS HEALTH WILL CONTINUE

TO BE GOOD. I LIFT TOM PUCKET UP
TO YOU LORD. AMEN.

6-24-96
Dear Heavenly Father, Lord
thank you for being so
faithful and true. You
are such an awesome
God.

6-26-96
Dear Heavenly Father, Lord
please forgive me for
even thinking of trying
to make Chad jealous.
That was so wrong of
me. Then when Tony
tried to make Chad jealous
I got mad. I had no
right because I thought
the same thing. It was
good to see Chad again.
We only talked for about
45 min. but that's better
then nothing. I pray for
his relationship with
you Lord. He is not doing
very well. I pray you
will put a flame of

desire to fall in love
with you Lord. I also
pray for he and his
girlfriends relationship.
Be the center of it
Lord. Please help chad
and i to get a firm
friendship growing.
I lift up Minette.
Lord help her to see
that there is a awesome
Christian guy and that
she should not have
settled for Brandon. Help
her to see your light.
Protect her heart Lord.
I love you so much.
Amen

85   1-2-96

TNL - applewood Baptist- Trevor
2 Timothy 4 1-5
· you only have one duty
- preach the word!
· you need to live your
life in consiotacy.
· be prepared to preach
· half of life is getting prepared
for what is to come.
· do you have seasons
with your faith?
- you always must be
prepared
· your life will go through
stages no matter what
will you stay consistent
through all those times?
1 if you correct go beside
and help them.
2 Rebuke
3 encourage
· only build eachother up
never tear them down.
ask for forgiveness

*Do not have your concert first and tune your instruments
afterward. Begin the day with God.*

JAMES HUDSON TAYLOR

- be a servant to those
you don't even know.
- put other peoples lives
before you.
4. be patient.
5. carefull instruction
are you willing to help
others to understand?
6 - they will turn away
Prov. 3:5-6
7 - 1. keep your head
2. endure life
- know things will change
3. being an evanglist
4. dischange all duties of
your ministry
* WHAT IS YOUR MINISTRF? *

7-3-96

DEAR HEAVENLY FATHER, LORD PLEASE
FORGIVE ME FOR NOT BEING THE
OBEDIANT SERVANT I SHOULD BE. I
TAKE YOU FOR GRANTED. LORD I'M
SORRY. I ASK THAT YOU WOULD HELP
ME TO BUILD MY FRIENDS AND OTHERS
UP AND NOT TO TEAR THEM DOWN. THAT
THE ONLY WORDS THAT COME OUT OF
MY MOUTH WOULD BE GLORIFYING TO
YOU. i LIFT TO YOU MINETTE. i PRAY
THAT YOU WILL BE THE MAIN FOCUS
POINT OF HER LIFE. HELP HER TO
UNDERSTAND SHE NEEDS TO LEAN
TO YOU IN EVERYTHING. i PRAY FOR
HER RELATIONSHIP WITH BRANDON.
I PRAY YOU WOULD PUT THE DESIRE
BACK INTO BRANDONS HEART TO
FALL IN LOVE WITH YOU. HELP
MINETTE TO KEEP HER MIND SET ON
NOT GETTING TO PHYSICAL W/BRANDON.
CONVICT THEM IF THEY ARE PUTTING
THEMSELFS IN A SITUATION THEY
SHOULD NOT BE IN. SAME GOES FOR
TONY-MELISSA AND DAN-STEF. MAKE
THEM REALIZE IT IS NOT GLORIFYING TO
YOU. YOU SHOULD BE THE CENTER OF

How great is the love the Father has lavished on us,
that we should be called children of God!

1 JOHN 3:1

ALL OF THERE RELATIONSHIPS. I ALSO
LIFT UP CHERYL AND HER TIME OF
TROUBLE. SHE IS HAVING A DIFFICULT
TIME WITH HER NON CHRISTIAN FRIENDS
I PRAY THAT THROUGH THIS TRIAL SHE
WILL GROW SO MUCH CLOSER TO YOU
AND NOT FALL. I PRAY FOR ALL OF
THE FRIENDS WHO DO NOT HAVE JOBS
YET. I ASK YOU WILL HELP THEM TO
BE PATIENT AND BLESS THEM WITH
A AWESOME JOB WHERE YOU CAN
USE THEM IN SO MANY AMAZING
WAYS. I PRAY FOR CHAD. KAREN TOLD
ME HE AND HIS GIRLFRIEND BROKE UP.
LORD PLEASE KEEP WATCH OVER HIM. HELP
HIM TO LOOK TO YOU! JESUS PLEASE
GIVE ME PATIENTS WITH THIS ENTIRE
THING WITH WANTING A BOYFRIEND SO
BADLY. I KNOW YOU HAVE SOMEONE
AWESOME PLANNED FOR ME AND I
NEED TO ~~BE~~ LEARN TO PUT ALL OF
MY TRUST IN YOU. YOU KNOW WHAT
YOU ARE DOING. I PRAY FOR TONIGHT.
MINETTE IS HAVING A GET TOGETHER.

I ASK THAT THINGS WILL BE FINE AND
THAT EVERYONE WILL GET ALONG WITH
EACH OTHER. I PRAY THAT IF AARON
GOES WE WOULD BE ABLE TO TALK
AND GET TO KNOW ONE ANOTHER BETTER.
I WOULD LIKE TO GET TO BE GOOD
FRIENDS. HE SEEMS TO BE RIGHT
WITH YOU AND THAT IS SO ENCOURAGING
TO KNOW. I PRAY THAT IF HE IS
GOING THROUGH ANY TROUBLESOME
TIME YOU WOULD BLESS HIM IN
THE END. I PRAY FOR MELISSA AND
HER TRIP TO WHALES. I PRAY SHE
WILL ALLOW YOU TO SHINE THROUGH
HER AND THAT SHE WILL GIVE ALL
OF THE GLORY TO YOU AND THAT
SHE WILL NOT TAKE ANY OF THE CREDIT
FOR HERSELF. HELP TO BE A GROWING
EXPERIENCE FOR HER. LORD PLEASE
HELP THE ENTIRE GROUP TO COME
CLOSER TO YOU AND MAKE US
DIFFERENT FROM OTHERS AROUND US.
LET PEOPLE SEE THAT WE ARE LIVING
FOR YOU AND WE LOVE YOU WITH
ALL OF OUR HEARTS. SHOW US WE
NEED TO BE SERVANTS FOR YOU. BLESS
THE TIME WE HAVE TOGETHER. I ♥ U. AMEN

7-5-96

Dear Lord Jesus, I thank you so much for being such an awesome God. I pray for Tony and Stefani. Stef. has so much bitterness towards Tony. Once they start talking again Stef. gets mad at him. Lord help her to see that he is her brother in Christ and that she needs to treat him with respect. I also pray for Stef and her relationship with you. I think she has fallen so far from you. I'm not sure but by her actions- flipping Tony off, the words coming out of her mouth that I will not repeat and her negative attitude. She has also been doing too much physical things with Dan. They

have done so much
together its insane. Lord
please convict the both
of them to not do any
more of that until they
are married. That goes for
Melissa and Tony also.
I'm not sure if they're
gone far or not and I
are not to know. It is
so heart breaking to
see all of my christian
friends behaving as
though they are not
christians. It must be
100 times worse for you
to see it Lord. The entire
group of friends are
pleasing the devil and
not you. I'm not saying
I'm any better because
I too have pleased the
devil and not you by
some of my actions and
words. We need to be
glorifying you Lord in
everything we do. Give

us an opportunity as a
group to see we have
all fallen and need to
come back to you and
be a light for you. Lord
please help me right now.
I don't believe I got
accepted into metro. Jeff
got a letter today saying
he was accepted. I'm
about to break down into
tears but I can't because
I'm at work. This makes
me feel so dumb. Not
only do I feel ugly, can't
get a boyfriend I can't
even get into metro.
Everyone I know has got
accepted to metro. It is
the easiest school to get
in, yet my grades are
so bad I can't even get
in. What is my problem.
Why do I feel as if
nobody wants me? I
know it's satan the sad
thing is, I'm believing

him. This is probably a test to see if I will still keep putting my trust in you and you alone. Help me Lord to not get down on myself. I know you will put me where you want me and I need to be patient. Help me to be patient. I lift up Jim and and the other people that work for him. I pray they will all come to know you in a personal way. I ask you to be with Yoanne. She cut her finger today. Help her to get some rest. I pray for Melissas trip to Whales. Start preparing the hearts of the people they will be witnessing

What makes humility so desirable is the marvelous thing it does to us; it creates in us a capacity for the closest possible intimacy with God.

MONICA BALDWIN

to. I pray for the health of all the people who are going to whales. Help them to remember they need to give all the glory to you. I pray for Cherye Lord. Take all of her burdens and give her the strength to help her grow closer to you. Lord please be with minette. Allow her to know if she should continue to be with Brandon or not. They are already talking about marriage. You know who they will marry. Help them to be patient. If they do want to get married may it be with the right intentions behind it. Lord I pray for my mom. She is so awesome and yet with my PMS or whatever I'm not very kind to her. Help

83

me to show her how much I do love her and for all the great things she has done for me. I thank you so much for her God. You couldn't have blessed me more with a mother like her. Give her the strength to put up with all us kids I know we are all such pains. I also thank you for my father. He is such a great dad. I pray you will heal his back and allow him to function okay. I thank you so much for Kari. She is a good sister. She is always there to talk to me when ever and shes always willing to give things to me. I pray she will come to have a personal relationship with you.

Do not be afraid, little flock, for your Father has been
pleased to give you the kingdom.

LUKE 12:32

I pray for aaron Smith
and his family. They are
moving into there new
house. Help them to have
a safe and great move.
Lord as Jeff is thinking
of moving to missouri
I pray you will do
whats in your will.
If he does move help
my parents deal with
it. I pray that if he
does move he won't get
into drugs or drinking.
Help him to grow and
get to know his true
self. I pray for Chad.
I still don't know where
his at in his relationship
with you. I pray that
he will get the desire to
fall in love with you.
I lift up Ranell and
melinda. From what

I understand Ranell and
Charles are talking again.
He up and left her about
2 months ago. Well now
his back. I also heard
she has been drinking
a lot more. I pray she
will soon come back
to you! I have not
talked with Melinda. I
also pray she will soon
come back to you Lord.
Help the both of them
to forgive Minette and
Stefani for what ever
they did to upset them.
You know there hearts
Lord. I love you so much
Jesus. Make me to be
a light for you. amen.
7-8-96

DEAR HEAVENLY FATHER—I THANK YOU
SO MUCH FOR THE FRIENDS YOU
HAVE BLESSED ME WITH I LIFT
EVERY SINGLE ONE OF THEM UP TO
YOU. MINETTE, STEFANI, MELISSA, KAREN,
AMY, TRISHA, NAT, CHERYL, AVERY, BRANDON,

TONY, DAN, KEVIN, PAT, AARON, STACY,
NANCY AND EVERYBODY ELSE. YOU
KNOW WHO THEY ARE. I ASK YOU
WOULD COMFORT THEM IN THEIR
NEEDS AND PROTECT THEM. I PRAY
FOR THEIR RELATIONSHIP WITH YOU.
I THINK A LARGE PORTION OF
THEM ARE FAR FROM YOU LORD.
HELP THEM TO REALIZE THEY NEED
TO COME TO YOU IN EVERYTHING.
PUT THE DESIRE BACK IN THEIR
HEARTS TO FALL IN LOVE WITH YOU.
I PRAY FOR CALVARY CHURCH
YESTERDAY PASTOR CURTIS RESINED
FROM BEING PASTOR. I DON'T KNOW
IF THATS GOOD OR BAD. BUT IT WAS
IN YOUR WILL BECAUSE YOU LET IT
HAPPEN. HE WAS ONLY HERE AT
CALVARY FOR ABOUT A YEAR. I PRAY
YOU WILL BLESS OUR CHURCH WITH
A PASTOR WHOSE FOCUS IS ON YOU
AND NOT ON THE PEOPLE. I PRAY
FOR THE CURTIS "FAMILY". LAY YOUR
HAND UPON THEM AND HELP THEM
TO COME TO YOU IN THIS TIME OF
NEED. HELP THEM NOT TO LOOSE
SIGHT OF YOU. BLESS WHO EVER

COMES IN TO GIVE THE SERMONS. I
PRAY FOR THE CHURCH AS A WHOLE.
THERE IS A LOT GOING ON IN THERE
THAT NOBODY KNOWS ABOUT. THE ELDERS
ARE KEEPING THINGS TO THEMSELVES.
THEY ARE NOT GOOD THINGS. LORD
TAKE CONTROL OVER OUR CHURCH.
MAKE THE ELDERS PUT YOU FIRST
AND NOT THE MONEY AND THE
NUMBER OF PEOPLE WE HAVE EACH
WEEK. I PRAY THAT MINETTES INTERVIEW
WENT WELL TODAY AND IF BE IN
YOUR WILL LORD ALLOW HER TO GET
THE JOB. IF YOU HAVE OTHER PLANS FOR
HER HELP HER TO SEE THAT. MAY YOUR
WILL BE DONE. I ALSO PRAY FOR
KAREN. LORD BLESS HER WITH A JOB
THAT YOU KNOW YOU COULD USE HER
THE MOST. I PRAY ABOUT SCHOOL LORD.
I WOULD LIKE TO GO TO METRO SO
LORD IF IT BE IN YOUR WILL PLEASE
LET ME RECIEVE SOMETHING THIS
WEEK IN THE MAIL TELLING ME I DID
GET IN. HELP ME TO BE PATIENT
BECAUSE I'M GETTING RESTLESS. I GOT
A LETTER FROM CHAD TODAY I HAVE
NOT READ IT YET. I JUST PRAY WE

CAN START A FRIENDSHIP THAT IS
BASED ON YOU LORD. I PRAY THAT
HE WILL GROW CLOSER TO YOU LORD.
I'M NOT SURE IF HE IS STILL
USING BAD LANGAUGE BUT I PRAY
THAT SOMEHOW HE WOULD READ
EPHESIANS 4:29 ABOUT DO NOT LET
ANY UNWHOLESOME TALK COME OUT
OF YOUR MOUTH. GRANTED THE TALK
THAT COMES OUT OF MY MOUTH
IS NOT THAT OF BUILDING OTHERS
UP. HELP ME LORD TO LET THE
WORDS THAT COME OUT OF MY
MOUTH LIFT THE OTHER UP. YOU ARE
SUCH AN AWESOME GOD LORD. HELP
ME YIELD TO YOU IN ALL-

7-10-96

Dear Heavenly Father, Lord
thank you so much for
being faithful. You are
such an awesome God.
I heard back from
metro yesterday and I
did get accepted. I know
if I wait you will
answer my prayer. I
know you always answer

82

my prayer, it just may
be not what I want
to hear. Well I read Chads
letter. Lord I lift him
up to you. After he got
back from Getaway he
went and partied for
3 days straight and drank.
Help me to be a witness
to him Lord. He does not
seem to be where he
should be. I thank you
so much for TW and
Trevor. It is so amazing
how much it's helped
me out spiritually. I
pray for all my friends
and myself. We have
not finished the race
yet, and we have just
all stopped. Work through
me Jesus. Help me to
yield and to be a on-
going soldier who will

*God loves us the way we are
but He loves us too much to leave us that way.*

LEIGHTON FORD

finish the race. I would like to be a silent wittness to all of my friends so they to see that they need to fight the good fight and to not give up so easily. I pray as I talk to Melissa tonight Lord that her heart will be softned to what I have to say to her about her and Tony being too physical in their relationship. Give me the words to say so I don't come across being judgemental. I would like to lift up the girl from TN. You know who she is. Comfort her Lord. Help her to see she needs to glorify you in everything. She has had a tough life. I'm not sure if Melissa and I confronting Tierra

about it was the best. But
we did it and now we
know why she is allowed
to dress the way she
does. Please help Trevor to
understand we did it out
of love and not to judge
her. I know he probably
knows because I told him
3 times we were not
judging her. I just get so
worried about people
thinking I'm judging
them b/c of my friends
getting mad at me for
telling them basically
what I think. I love
you Lord. Amen.

7-12-96
Dear Lord Jesus, I thank you
so much for blessing me with
my family. I'm a little worried
about Krista Lord. She does not
seem to be happy at all. She
hardly goes out with her friends
anymore. And she is also getting
in to deep with this whole diet

I will not forget you! See, I have engraved you
on the palms of my hands.

ISAIAH 49:15,16

thing. She never eats anymore.
Granted I also have been
doing the slim fast shakes,
but she is going out of control.
She never eats with the
family anymore. Lay your hand
on her Lord. If she is developing
a eating disorder, help her to
see she was made in your
way. I also pray for Kari. She
seems to be drinking more
these days. Keep her safe Lord.
Keep watch over my family. Dad
seems to be taking Wally's
death hard. He knew Wally from
when he was 15. Comfort him
in this time of need. I pray
that he will come closer to
you during all of this. Thank
you for blessing my family
and I the way you have.
Help all of us to yeild to you
Lord. You are such an
awesome God. I pray for

Minette. She found out a few days ago that her parents are not going to pay any of her way for college. She has no money and no job. You know what you are doing Lord. I think she is having doubts about even going to school now. She kept telling me that nobody in her family has gone to college and they are living comfortably. Help her to make the right choices Lord. Continue to make me a silent witness at work. I pray that through you working through me, some of the packers for Jim may come to know you. And Jim himself. I pray for all of us in the group who are going to be starting our first year of college. I pray that we will continue to love you and come so much closer to you. We will all be leaving our comfort zone and starting over. Let the

transition be an easy one for
us all. And if it be th your
will Lord we will all continue
to stay friends. I pray for
Stefani she needs to soften
her heart and love those
around her. Especially Tony
and the fellow christians at
our church. It's seems to me
that she always has to be mad
at someone. I don't know why
she is so angry with Tony,
only you know. Help her to see
that it is childish.

7-24-96
Dear Heavenly Father, Lord
please protect my entire
self. satan is telling me
all of these awful lies.
Protect me Lord, fill me
with your cleansing. In
the name of the Lord
Jesus Christ, satan get.
Your way is the only
way and I want your
will be done. Help me
to be more like you.

82

I want the fire in me
to be a roaring fire not
just a single flame. you
are my rock and my
fortress in you will I
trust. Help me Lord to
be patient in all areas.
Especially the guy era.
I do pray Lord you will
bless me with such an
awesome Godly man. I
know I need to be
patient but I would like
one soon just so I have
the opportunity to grow
with him. And also
experience the growth in
you with another person
Take control Lord. I lift
up Melissa and her
mom. They are in
Whales right now with
others on a mission
trip. I pray that you
are speaking through
them and helping them
all grow closer to you.

I pray that this trip will do something so awesome for Melissa and that she will reevaluate some of her actions from the past. Same goes for everyone.

I also pray for the Spences from Church. Lord I pray that you will use them in so many awesome ways as they translate and move into a different environment. Use them to the best ways you can. I lift Kari up to you Lord. She is going through some troublesome times right now. Bless her Lord. Help her to see your light.

I pray that there would not be any rumors spread. I pray that you will give her the right thing to do

with her situation.
With the situation that's
going on with Minette's
mom and step dad. You
know what it is. Who
knows if you will bring
divorce into the picture
if it helps for one of
them to come to know
you Lord let your will
be done. Help Minette,
Tommy and Trent as
their parents don't get
along as for Minette
getting this job at the
F.B.I. You know where
you want her Lord. I pray
that by your grace she
will somehow get the
money to go to ccu. She
is not going now b/c
she has no money. She
won't go to Metro for some
reason so she is not

going to school at all.
I pray for all of my
friends who have no
desire to go to college.
Karen, Michelle and I
believe Tony. Maybe you
have something better
planned for their life.
I just pray that their
reason is self centered.
Let it be God centered.
I pray for Janet Irwin.
She is our cousin. I
am not exactly sure
what she has done in
her past. Lord please
protect her. I'm glad she
broke up with her mormon
boyfriend. Help her to fall
in love with you. I
also pray for the rest
of the cousins in Missouri.
I don't think they are
doing to well. Only you
know. Through something
make your presence known.
I lift up Breanna. Prepare

her heart Lord for someone
who will speak to her
about you. Soften her heart
so she will be willing
to listen. I pray that do
we all start school in
about a month that you
would stay the center of
attention and that we may
grow closer to you! I pray
my focus will be on you
first and above all other
things. I also ask for the
energies and the patience
and dicipline once school
starts. I thank you so
much for Krista Lord. Even
though we don't get along
all the time she is
such a great sister. I
know I say I can't
wait until she leaves,
but I know as soon
as she does I will
miss her like crazy.
I also thank you for my
mom, dad, Karl, Jeff & Nick.

I will put my law in their minds and write it on their hearts.
I will be their God and they will be my people.

JEREMIAH 31:33

Mom and dad do so much for me and I take it for granted. They love me and yet I don't show it enough that I love them in return. They are the best parents a kid could ever ask for. Kari, Jeff and Rick are great! They are so good to me and I need to start repaying them in return. I love my family so much. I take them for granted too often. Even Grandma Helen. She has been a terrific grandma. Thank you for blessing me with such a great family. Yesterday was Steffs birthday. Tonight she is having a party. I pray that all goes well with that. I thank you for

Stef. I pray she will soon forgive Tony for whatever he did to her. I lift up Brandon, Pat, Tony, Aaron, Jeremy, Dan, A.J., Adam, and Andy. Lord make them become more like you. I pray they will put you the center of their relationships. And also the girls; Minette, Stef, Melissa, Trisha, Karen, Amy, Nat, Avery, Cheryl. You are such an awesome God. Thank you for your many blessings Lord. I love you with all my heart, soul and mind. In your sons name amen.

7-31-96
Dear Gracious Heavenly Father, Lord protect me. Put your healing arms around me. I thank you so much for my parents Lord. I love them so much and take them for granted too often. I get upset

with them over the silliest
things. comfort them now
Lord as they are going
through all these changes.
if you want us to have
this house open a door
but if not that you
would bless us with
what ever you want. I lift
up Ted Bowman to you
Lord. He is one of my
dads friends who is in
the hospital. If he is
not a christian I pray
he may come to know
you in the next few
days if he is not going
to make it. Use Harry
and my dad as a light.
I pray for this women
who is in here at the
Shipping connection is a
lesbian show her the
light Lord. I pray for
all my friends. I have
not seen them for a
week. Today I woke up

with a strange feeling. I
miss all my friends so
much. I never thought
I would and its only
been a week. Are you
trying to tell me Something

8-14-96
Dear Heavenly Father, God I
desire to know you and love
you with all of my heart.
I want that to be my
only desire. I don't need
all the earthly things to
fill the desires because
I have you. Please forgive
me God from hiding
from you. I've been
fooling myself by believing
I am right on with
you but I'm not. I'm
far from it. By my actions,
my thoughts, my unkind
words that come out of
my mouth etc. I want
your love to shine through
me. I want to be in the
light. I want to love others

and treat others with love
and respect. I want others
to see that you are within
me by the fruits I spread.
God I repent of all the
thoughts that were not glorifying
to you. Convict me God when
ever they start to enter my
mind. You are such an
awesome God and I tend
to take that for granted.
Help me God to not have
such a complaining heart.
Don't let me think of
myself as having the
worst time every day.
Let me think of others
and be grateful you have
blessed me with such
wonderful people in my
life. Thank you God for doing
them to talk about all
these things so you could
show me where you want
me to be and where I
would like to be. Use my
God. I pray for all my

friends who leave this week
for school. Dan and Aaron
leave today. God I ask that
you will protect them from
Satans lies. Help them
to look for you in all they
do God. I also pray for Pat,
Jake, Chrissy, Jeff, Amy, Theresa,
Kevin, Krista, Trisha, Adam,
Andy, and whom ever else
is leaving in the next
few weeks God don't let them
fall in the trap of being
accepted. If they have the
temptation to drink that
they would realize its not
glorifying to you. I pray for
Jeff God. I don't know why
but I think he is
smoking. I know I think
this a lot. Last night I woke
up to the smell of
cigarette smoke comeing in
my window. who Only you

*Our love for God is tested
by whether we seek Him or His gifts.*

RALPH SOCKMAN

know if it was Jeff or not
Lord, but if it is I pray
that you will show him that
he should not be doing it.
He wants so much to fit
in somewhere. He has so
many personalities. He
transforms to the people he
hangs around. I lift up
Kanell. Lord please use
me to bring her close to
you again. As school begins
let us talk more. I pray
for Milinda. She is so
much into drugs now it's
not even funny. She has
no desire to go to school
or anything. Lord show her
the light. Allow her to see
she needs to come back to
you. Lord be with Karen as she
starts this job on Mon.
And if you would like for
Minette to get this job
at the FBI help her to be
patient.
I pray for everybody in

the group. We have all fallen
so much from you Lord. Put
the desire in all of our hearts
to come closer to you Lord.
Thank you for being such
an awesome forgiving God!
In your sons name Amen.
8-15-96

DEAR HEAVENLY FATHER, LORD PLEASE
GIVE ME THE PATIENCE TO DEAL
WITH THE PEOPLE I HANG AROUND.
THEY HAVE ALL CHANGED SO MUCH.
EVERY WORD THAT COMES OUT
OF THEIR MOUTH IS AWFUL. LAST
NIGHT WAS PAT'S GOING AWAY
PARTY. ALL OF THE GUYS WERE
BEING SO DISRESPECTFUL TO YOU
LORD. THE WORST THING WAS
THEY ARE ALL IN A RELATIONSHIP
WITH YOU. I HAD NO DESIRE
TO BE AROUND THEM. SO MANY
CHRISTIANS ARE GOING IN
THE WRONG DIRECTION. I PRAY
FOR EVERYBODY IN THE WORLD
WHO HAS HAD A PERSONAL
RELATIONSHIP WITH YOU. I PRAY
THAT THEY WILL HAVE THE DESIRE

Above all else, guard your heart,
for it is the wellspring of life.

PROVERBS 4:23

TO KNOW YOU. I PRAY FOR PAT
LORD. HE LEAVES TODAY FOR
SCHOOL. I DID NOT KNOW HOW
MUCH I WOULD MISS HIS
FRIENDSHIP UNTIL I AM NOW
FACED WITH IT. HE HAS BEEN
SUCH A GREAT FRIEND OVER
THESE YEARS HE'S ALLWAYS
BEEN THERE TO TALK TO ME
ABOUT GUYS OR WHAT EVER.
LORD PUT YOUR HAND UPON
HIM AND KEEP HIM UNDER
YOUR WING. I PRAY WE WILL
CONTINUE TO BE FRIENDS
WHILE HE GOES AWAY FOR
SCHOOL. HELP ALL OF US WHO
ARE GOING TO HAVE CLOSE
PEOPLE LEAVE FOR SCHOOL.
I PRAY THEY WILL LEAN TO
YOU FOR EVERYTHING THEY
NEED. THANK YOU LORD I LOVE
YOU WITH MY WHOLE HEART.
IN YOUR NAME. AMEN.

8-16-96

Dear Heavenly Father, Lord
please calm my spirit.
I am getting emotional
with having all my
friends leaving. The two
that have left already
that I will miss greatly
are Pat and Jake. I love
them so much. They
have been there for me
time and time again. Lord
I ask that you will
continue to make our
friendships grow even
though they are in another
state. Thank you Lord for
blessing me with such
wonderful friends. Prepare
me for when the rest
of my friends have to
leave. I don't understand
why all these christians
are falling into the way
of the Lord. I lift up
Shannon and Andy. Jake
told me she is pregnant

It is so hard to hear that because I know that they had such an awesome relationship with you. I also heard that a few of the guys I know who are christians have started to drink and do drugs. I know it's not any of my business it's just so sad. Lord you must be coming back soon. I pray for this school year Lord. Help everyone to concentrate on you and their studies. And as temptations arise they will not do anything that is against you because you are the supreme being. Show us all your greatness. Thank you again Lord for blessing me with such great friends. I pray we will always stay close and pray for one another. In your name amen.

8-21-94

Dear Lord Jesus, Thank you
so much for Trevor, the
pastor of TNL. You have
taght me so many things
through Trevor. Last night
I brought Jeff to TNL. Trevor
said something about mormons.
I talked to Trevor after
the sermon. I pray that
he does not think I hate
him. The only time I
basically talk to him it's
about something negative.
I hope he understands
my letter I wrote him
today and let him know
how much I do care
for him. Thank you Lord
for blessing Trevor with
the spiritual gift you did.
He has helped many
people out. Thank you Lord.
I pray Jeff will come
back one day to TNL. I
pray for Stef as she
leaves on Sat. Allow them

to have a safe and comfertable trip. Thank you Lord for being such an awesome God. Help me to become more like you. I love you. In your sons name amen.

8-23-96

DEAR LORD JESUS, WELL TOMORROW STEFANI AND KRISTA LEAVES. I KNOW I HAVE NOT GOTTEN ALONG WITH KRISTA ALL THAT WELL THIS SUMMER. I DON'T KNOW WHAT ARE DEALS WERE. I PRAY FOR HER NEXT YEAR AT SCHOOL. BLESS HER IN MANY WAYS. I PRAY FOR STEP LORD. AS SHE BEGINS U.BALL KEEP A GAURD OVER HER MOUTH. I ASK THAT YOU WILL SOFTEN HER HEART. MAKE HER INTO A LOVING, CAREING, FORGIVING PERSON. I PRAY SHE WILL FORGIVE TONY FOR ALL HE HAS DONE TO HER. LET HER SEE YOUR AWESOME-NESS AND YOUR FORGIVENESS AND PUT THE DESIRE IN HER HEART TO FOLLOW YOU AND ALL YOUR COMMANDS. I PRAY THAT YOU

WILL GIVE ME THE MOTIVATION THIS
NEXT SCHOOL YEAR TO ACTUALLY
KEEP UP WITH MY STUDIES AND TO
NOT SLACK OFF. KEEP ME MOTIVATED
LORD. WE LOOKED AT A HOUSE LAST
NIGHT. IT WAS A NICE HOUSE. I LIKED
IT A LOT. LORD IF YOU WANT
US THERE, OPEN UP A DOOR TO THE
WAY WE COULD AFFORD TO DO IT.
AND IF THIS IS NOT YOUR WILL
WE WILL UNDERSTAND. HELP US TO
YIELD TO YOU LORD. LORD PLEASE
CALM MY SPIRIT. I AM UPSET WITH
MELISSA. SHE HAS LIED TO ME FOR I
DON'T KNOW HOW LONG. JUST ABOUT
SMALL THINGS. HER AND TONY HAVE
GONE WAY FAR IN THEIR RELATIONSHIP.
THE PHYSICAL SIDE OF IT. SHE HAS TOLD
ME THEY HAVE NOT GONE FAR. WHEN
SHE TALKS TO STEF AND MINETTE
SHE TELLS THEM THEY HAVE AND
SHE DOES NOT WANT TO TELL ME
BECAUSE SHE DOES NOT WANT ME
TO LOOSE RESPECT FOR HER. WELL

One of God's specialties is to make somebodies
out of nobodies.

HENRIETTA MEARS

IT'S TOO LATE. ONE BECAUSE SHE IS
GOING SO FAR WITH TONI AND TWO
BECAUSE SHE IS LIEING TO ME.
SHE HAS CHANGED FROM THE TIME
HER AND TONI HAVE GOTTEN TOGETHER
UNTIL NOW. SHE IS NOT THE SAME
PERSON I KNOW. GRANTED I'VE NEVER
BEEN IN A RELATIONSHIP BUT I KNOW
I DON'T WANT TO FALL INTO THAT
TRAP BECAUSE I AM NOT MARRIED
AND IT IS NOT GLORIFYING TO YOU
LORD I'M GOING TO STAY AWAY
FROM MELISSA FOR AWHILE. IF SHE
ASKS ME WHY I WON'T LIE. LORD
IF YOU DON'T WANT ME TO DO
IT THAT WAY I WON'T. LORD MAKE
ME MORE LIKE YOU. I KNOW I'M
NOT PERFECT BUT I WANT TO
STRIVE TO BE. I WANT TO FALL
IN LOVE WITH YOU. I WANT MY
ENTIRE LIFE TO BE BASED ON YOU
ALONE. PROTECT ME FROM ALL LIES
SATAN TRIES TO TELL ME. YOUR
LOVE OVERPOWERS THAT SO MUCH
MORE. HELP ME TO YIELD TO YOU
LORD. I LOVE YOU SO MUCH LORD.
I NO LONGER WANT TO HIDE FROM

YOU. THANK YOU LORD JESUS FOR
FORGIVING ME ALL THE TIMES YOU
HAVE. I LOVE YOU. AMEN.
8-26-96

Dear Lord Jesus, thank you
so much for using
minette to show me
that I need to lean to
you and not my friends.
She helped me realize
that I should not rely
on my friends and I
need to rely on you. I
pray for the friendship I
have with Melissa. I
told her last night I
was tired of her always
lieing to me. I forgive
her but I don't think
things are even close
to being worked out. I
was too harsh with
her. God please forgive
me. I went about it
in the wrong way. I
was pointing a finger
when I shouldn't

> He who has the Son has life; he who does not have
> the Son of God does not have life.
>
> 1 JOHN 5:12

have been.

9-9-96

Dear Lord Jesus Thank you for having that program on this morning about ~~repentance~~ repentance. Help me to keep that state of mind Lord. Please forgive me Lord for talking bad about people behind their backs. I repent of this Lord. Make me more like you. I pray for Minette. She is having a difficult time with her and Brandon being "split up." She has hatred in her. I also pray for her relationship with you. Put the flame of desire back into her heart Lord. She use to be one of the only

people I could go to about
you Lord. Work in her
life Lord. Help her to
be in the light. I also
pray that you would
put the desire back
in Brandons heart.
Help him to realize he
needs you. I lift up
Tony and Melissa's
relationship to you Lord.
They have made the
descion to not have any
pysicalness in their
relationship. I pray
they will continue to
have that mind set.
Thank you so much.
Lord for mending Melissa
and my relationship.
I pray for all of us
that we would be
in the light and every-
day become more like
you. I pray for Karen.
She may go to a concert
on Friday. I pray she

would not go because
I'm sure there will
be drugs and it may
tempt her. Protect her
Lord! Lord I feel as
though Jim, my boss
has something

9-18-96

Dear Lord Jesus, please
forgive me for not
being the obediant
child I need to be.
You give me so many
opportunities, yet I just
let them pass by.
You are such an
awesome God. Lord I
pray that you would
bring me someone
special into my life.
You know what I mean.
I often take matters
into my own hands.
Lord help me to be
patient. I also have a
problem with jealousy.
I'm very jealous of

Minette and those who
I think are prettier
than I. Thats why I
get intimidated. I pray
Lord you would some
how give me confidence.
I pray for Pat Lord.
He and Krissy broke up.
I pray that they
would both lean to
you for their comfort.
I lift Nancy Astor to
you Lord. She is spiritually
dry. Give her the food
she needs to become alive
in you again. That goes
for all of us Lord
Lord if you want me
to help out with
Student Venture open a
door for me if you
feel it is something
I am not ready for
then dont. You know
where you want me
Lord. I will go where
ever you direct me.

I pray for Jeff. I don't think he would wants anything with you. You know what you are doing Lord.

Last night at TVC I saw Matt Taylor. You know what is going on. I pray you would soften both of our hearts Lord. You are the only one who knows whats going on. I thank you so much for TVC and Trevor Lord. You have used him so much to others and to me. He is such an awesome gift from you. Lord I want to be in the light as you are in the light. Give me the ability to shine for you Lord Jesus you have done so many amazing things in these past few years. Thank you. I love you with my entire being. amen